S0-AUO-766

A LIGUORI CLASSIC

Selected Writings
and Prayers of

Saint
Alphonsus

Adapted for Modern Readers by
John Steingraeber, C.SS.R.
With an Introduction by
R. J. Miller, C.SS.R.

Liguori
ONE LIGUORI DRIVE
LIGUORI MO 63057-9999
314.464.2500

Imprimi Potest:
Daniel Lowery, C.SS.R.
Provincial, St. Louis Province
Redemptorist Fathers

Imprimatur:
+ George J. Gottwald
Vicar General of St. Louis

ISBN 0-7648-0025-6
Library of Congress Catalog Card Number:
97-71961

Copyright © 1997, Liguori Publications
Printed in the United States of America
97 98 99 00 01   5 4 3 2 1

This book was previously published under the title Love Is Prayer; Prayer Is Love, Liguori Publications, copyright © 1973, Liguori, Missouri.

Cover design by Christine Kraus

table of contents

CONFORMITY TO THE WILL OF GOD

THOUGHTS ON THE INCARNATION
(pp. 91-122)

THOUGHTS ON THE HOLY SPIRIT
(pp. 123-137)

THE GLORIES OF MARY

PRAYERS OF ST. ALPHONSUS

tribute to an extraordinary doctor

Alphonsus Liguori was born in Naples in 1696 and died near there in 1787. He was canonized in 1839; named a Doctor of the Church in 1871; and made patron of confessors and moral theologians in 1950.

He deserves to be called "extraordinary" if only for the fact that he is the only professional moral theologian ever to be canonized a saint. He would seem to deserve it also for the influence he has had on the development of doctrine in the Church, and the power which he still has to speak to the hearts of the people, as likewise for the surprising way in which his personality and teaching are relevant to the needs of modern man.

St. Alphonsus systematized moral theology as part of his wider pastoral activity for the good of souls. All of his books — and he wrote about a hundred of them, ranging from the scientific to the devotional — are aimed at practice rather

5

than theory. They were the outgrowth of his actual contact with people; he labored for more than 40 years as a parish missioner and director of consciences. In fact, he had a kind of horror of what he called empty subtleties. It was no ambition of his to be a philosopher, remotely expounding the theory of Christian living; rather, he is a strategist, laying down the actual battle plans for victory in the strife.

Even in his own lifetime his books went through many editions, and won him an international reputation. They have continued spreading ever since. Careful checking has established that in the less than 200 years since his death there have been more than 20,000 editions of his works. This makes Alphonsus Liguori extraordinary in still another way, as the second best seller of all time, ancient or modern, sacred or secular. Only the Bible has outsold him.

He is the only professional moral theologian ever to be canonized, and that fact almost cost him his canonization. The devil's advocate brought it up as a bar to the admission of his cause. He pointed out that Alphonsus Liguori, as a moral theologian, has covered in his books much of the field of human activity. To canonize such a man, he warned the judges in the case, would be to lend the authority of the Catholic Church to everything he ever wrote on the subject of morality. With this in mind, he demanded that, over and above the ordinary scrutiny given to the writings of any candidate for sanctity, the works of Alphonsus Liguori be subjected to a second and far more searching examination. The judges — and the pope — listened, agreed, examined; and then gave their *unanimous* approval to the doctrine of Alphonsus Liguori.

As a matter of fact, the Church seems to entertain no fears whatsoever as to the doctrine of this particular moral theologian. In a relatively few years, she went on to dignify him with still higher tokens of her esteem. She admitted him to the exclusive company of Doctors of the Church — again, the only professional moralist in that august band. Not so many years later (especially in view of the old truth that "Rome moves slowly"), she raised him higher still: naming him patron, that is, model and guide, for all confessors and all moral theologians to the end of time.

Moreover, since he first published his *Moral Theology*, practically every Roman pontiff from Benedict XIV until now has come out with special official tributes of praise for his doctrine. Then, too, when difficult questions were proposed to the Holy See for solution, time and again the official answer given by the teaching Church was: Consult and follow the teaching of St. Alphonsus Liguori.

Nor is it only in the field of moral theology that the Church looks up to him as a master. According to the official decree of July 7, 1871, by which he was named a Doctor of the Church, she sees in him an outstanding champion on whom she can depend whenever there is need for a man of action to defend her rights and to lead people to God. For one thing, says Pius IX, "He completely destroyed the pernicious error of Jansenism." Indeed, "He did much to confound every modern error." He was a champion of papal infallibility long before it was defined as a dogma of the Church. So, too, he championed the Immaculate Conception of the Blessed Virgin Mary. In matters of conscience, the decree goes on, amidst a welter of extreme opinions on counseling and moral guidance, Alphonsus Liguori blazed a trail which can be followed with perfect security by all counselors and directors of souls. In general, the decree credits him with the truly extraordinary achievement of having renewed in the Church the spirit of Christian piety.

Few saints, and surely no moral theologian, have been raised to such heights of trust and honor by the Catholic Church. She places Alphonsus Liguori in the select company of Aquinas and Augustine as a master who towers above the giants. His founder's statue in St. Peter's, Rome, occupies a position — such at least is the fond belief of his Redemptorist sons, rightfully proud of "our holy father Alphonsus" — which is in keeping with this view. As is well known, the canonized founders of religious orders, men and women, have each a gigantic statue in the niches which line the inner walls of the basilica. There are two rows of niches, one above the other. When Pope Gregory XVI was asked where the statue of St. Alphonsus should be placed, he indicated the upper niche at the sanctuary end of the church. "I want him near me," he said. But this brought St. Alphonsus directly above the Altar of the Chair, so called because it is surmounted by what tradition has held to be the original chair of St. Peter. The chair is now massively encased in ebony and bronze and sustained by the giant figures of four Doctors of the early Church: Sts. Athanasius, Ambrose, Augustine and John Chrysostom. The location of St. Alphonsus' statue has him quite literally "towering above the giants" even in St. Peter's, as he gazes down from his founder's niche devotedly, protectingly, on altar and chair, and the four giant Doctors of old.

It is the office of any Doctor of the Church to *teach the Catholic Church*. This does not mean that he adds any new truths to the original deposit of faith. It merely indicates that he has a special gift from God for bringing out the old truths more clearly — as part of the development of doctrine in the Church — and that he speaks with special force and charm to the hearts of the people.

St. Alphonsus has taught, and continues to teach, the Catholic Church in both of these ways. Various official pronouncements of the magisterium on matters both dogmatic and devotional owe much to his influence. When the First Vatican Council defined the infallibility of the pope, his treatise on the subject was on the table of the Council Fathers who worked to bring about the definition. His writings also helped prepare the way for the definition of the Immaculate Conception of the Blessed Virgin Mary and her Assumption into heaven. In the devotional field, he anticipated the action taken by popes in the 19th and 20th centuries by ardently promoting devotion to the rosary and to the Sacred Heart, and the practice of frequent Communion. It may even be said that many of the canons in the 1918 Code of Canon Law were anticipated by him, since he had thrashed them out pro and con at great length in his *Moral Theology.*

His gift for speaking to the hearts of the people is truly extraordinary. The record shows that there are really two classes of people for whom St. Alphonsus has a special appeal: the profoundly learned, who can appreciate beneath his deceptively simple style the range and depth of his genius; and the simple ordinary folk, who find in him a father speaking to their hearts. The superficial and mediocre can discover in him nothing to their taste.

A missionary in the interior of the Philippine Islands tells of an old lady in his parish who came begging him for a copy of

The Glories of Mary by St. Alphonsus, a translation in her native island tongue. She had loaned out her old copy, and could not get it back. Now she wanted another for herself. Placing her hand on her breast, she said: "It is a book that makes the heart warm!"

There must indeed be some kind of "incendiary" quality in his writings, to explain the fact that thousands of people, educated and uneducated alike, are still reading them every day; are still reciting his prayers; still feeling their hearts warmed with his fire. It is doubtful if there is any saint or Doctor of the Church whose writings and prayers are being used so widely today as those of St. Alphonsus.

Learned readers who try to probe the secret of his appeal find in him a set of striking contrasts. Massive erudition is combined with childlike devotion to the magisterium of the Church. He has the ardor of a poet, but also the calm and balanced reserve of a judge at law. His ardent love for God embraces a love for man that places him foremost in the campaign for human freedom.

His vast erudition is obvious, for instance, in the number of citations in his *Moral Theology*: 80,000 citations from 800 authors. And at the same time, despite his genius and his learning, he is humble as a child in his devotion to Rome. This is a combination rarely to be found.

Readers marvel still more at how a man

who could compose a work aflame with Christian mysticism like the *Visits to the Blessed Sacrament* could be the same man who weighs and balances so dispassionately and objectively the sordid extremes of human conduct treated in his *Moral Theology*. So too are they amazed that a saint with his life dedicated to the principle, "Give yourself entirely to God," can be the same man who devised and defended against all comers a moral system having for a leading principle, "A doubtful law does not bind."

To those who know St. Alphonsus well, learned and unlearned alike, he is a teacher with special relevance for our modern age. Pope Pius XII called him: "The Doctor for our age," and Pope Paul VI said: "This saint, more than other Doctors of the Church, seems to belong to our times." He has a personality and a teaching which meet the needs of an age in transition: an age of anti-intellectualism needs his spirit of solid learning; an age of rebellion needs his devoted loyalty to authority; an age of religious indifference needs his dedication to God; an age of hasty extremes needs his spirit of balanced judgment.

In the field of moral theology he has a special relevance today. Modern moral theology is beset with problems and confusion, largely stemming from *aggiornamento* and existentialism. But if the moral system which St. Alphonsus devised is examined carefully, it is found to meet in a surprisingly relevant manner the very heart of the problems of *aggiornamento* and existentialism. Students of Alphonsus should be well aware of this.

In practical, everyday life, Alphonsus continues to exercise his sway over the hearts of the people. They keep reading his works and using his prayers. The purpose of this volume, then, is to combine in one book an adaptation of some of his most popular writings. His old and faithful readers will appreciate this blending of their favorite passages and prayers. And new readers will be exposed to the wondrous healing power of this extraordinary Doctor.

R. J. Miller, C.SS.R.
Versailles, Kentucky

ımpoRtance of pRayeR

INTRODUCTION

I do not think I have written a more useful work than this one, in which I speak of prayer as a necessary and certain means of obtaining salvation and all the graces we need for it. If it were in my power, I would distribute a copy to every Catholic in the world in order to show him the absolute necessity of prayer for salvation. The absolute necessity of prayer is taught throughout the Holy Scriptures and by all the holy Fathers, but too often Christians are very careless in their practice of this great means of salvation.

Consequently, there is nothing which preachers, confessors, and spiritual books should insist upon with more warmth and energy than prayer. They teach many excellent means of keeping ourselves in the grace of God, such as avoiding occasions of sin, frequenting the sacraments, resisting temptations, hearing the Word of God, meditating on the eternal truths, and other means. But what if we forget to pray?

Without prayer, in most cases, all the meditations we make, all our resolutions, all our promises will be useless. If we do not pray, we shall be always unfaithful to the inspirations of God and to the promises we make him. Because to do good, to conquer temptations, to practice virtues, and to observe God's law, it is not enough to receive insight from God and to meditate and make resolutions. We require the actual assistance of God, and he does not give this assistance except to those who pray, and pray with perseverance.

When we are in danger and tempted to disobey God's law, prayer will obtain for us God's help and we shall be preserved from sin. But if in such moments we do not pray, we shall be lost.

I hope my readers may thank God for giving them this opportunity to think more deeply on the importance of prayer; for all adults who are saved are ordinarily saved by this single means of grace. I ask my readers to thank God, for surely it is a great mercy when he gives the light and grace to pray. I hope, then, that you, after reading this little work, will never from this day forward neglect to turn to God in prayer whenever you are tempted to offend him.

If you have ever had your conscience burdened with many sins, know that the cause of this has been the neglect of prayer and not asking God for help to resist the temptations which attacked you. And after reading this yourself, encourage your friends and neighbors to read it too.

I

NECESSITY, VALUE,
AND CONDITIONS OF PRAYER

St. Paul writes to Timothy: "First of all, I urge that petitions, prayers, intercessions, and thanksgiving be offered" (1 Tm 2:1). St. Thomas explains that prayer is the lifting up of the soul to God. Petition is that kind of prayer which begs for specific favors. Thanksgiving is the returning of thanks for benefits received, whereby we merit to receive greater favors. The word "prayer" is used here in its general meaning, which includes all its different forms and purposes.

A. Necessity of Prayer

God has so formed man that he himself is man's only strength. God has willed that whatever man has, or can have, should come entirely from the assistance of his grace. But this grace is not given in God's ordinary providence except to those who pray for it. So realizing on the one hand that we can do nothing without the assistance of grace, and on the other that this assistance is ordinarily only given by God to the man that prays, who does not see that prayer is absolutely necessary for our salvation? And although the first graces which come to us without any cooperation on our part — such as the call to faith or to penance — are granted by God even to those who do not pray, it is considered certain that the other graces, especially the gift of perseverance, are not granted except in answer to prayer.

In the ordinary course of providence, it is impossible for a Christian to be saved without recommending himself to God and asking for the graces necessary to salvation. St. Thomas teaches the same thing: "After Baptism, continual prayer is necessary to man, in order that he may enter heaven."

Our human weaknesses attack us from within, and the world and the devil attack us from without. The reason, then, which makes us certain of the necessity of prayer is this: In order to be saved, we must struggle and conquer. But without the divine assistance, we cannot resist the might of so many and so powerful enemies. Now this assistance is only granted through prayer. Therefore, without prayer there is no salvation. St. Thomas, in another place, says that whatever graces God has determined to give us, he will only give them if we pray for them. "Ask, and you will receive. Seek, and you will find" (Mt 7:7).

We are beggars, who have nothing but what God gives us. The Lord, says St. Augustine, desires and wills to pour forth his graces upon us, but will not give them except to him who prays. This is declared in the words, "Seek, and it shall be given you." He who does not seek, does not receive. St. John Chrysostom says: "As the body without soul cannot live, so the soul without prayer is dead . . . " Prayer is also called the food of the soul because the body cannot be supported without food, nor can the soul, says St. Augustine, be kept alive without prayer. All these comparisons used by the holy Fathers are intended to teach the absolute necessity of prayer for the salvation of everyone.

Prayer is the most necessary weapon of defense against our enemies. St. Thomas does not doubt that the reason for Adam's Fall was that he did not recommend himself to God when he was tempted. In darkness, distress, and danger, we have no other hope than to raise our eyes to God and with fervent prayers to beg his mercy to save us. Said King Jehoshaphat, "We are at a loss what to do, hence our eyes are turned toward you" (2 Chr 20:12). This also was David's practice, who could find no other means of safety from his enemies than continual prayer to God to deliver him from their traps: "My eyes are ever toward the Lord, for he will free my feet from the snare" (Ps 25:15).

"God does not command impossibilities; but by commanding he suggests you do what you can, and ask for what is beyond your strength; and he helps you, that you may be able." This is a famous text from St. Augustine which was afterward adopted and made a doctrine of faith by the Council of Trent. We cannot believe, the saint explains, that God would have imposed on us the observance of a law and then made the law impossible to keep. God knows that alone we are unable to observe all his commands. We can do the more difficult things only by means of the greater help which we can obtain by prayer.

Why has God commanded us to do things impossible to our natural strength? Precisely for this, says St. Augustine, that we may be led to pray for help to do what we cannot do alone. It is especially difficult for someone to resist temptations against purity without recommending himself to God when he is tempted. This type of temptation often seems to take away all light; it makes us forget all our meditations and good resolutions, induces us to disregard the truths of faith, and even almost causes us to lose fear of the divine punishments. When such temptation comes, the person who does not have recourse to God is lost. Chastity is a virtue which we do not have strength to practice unless God gives it to us, and God does not give this strength except to someone who asks for it. But whoever prays for it will certainly obtain it.

St. Francis of Assisi says that without prayer you can never hope to find good fruit in a soul. Sinners wrongly excuse themselves by saying that they have no strength to resist temptation. If you do not have this strength, why do you not ask for it? That is the reproof which St. James gives them: "You do not obtain because you do not ask" (Jas 4:2).

There is no doubt that we are too weak to resist the attacks of our enemies. But on the other hand it is certain that God is faithful. St. Paul says that he will not permit us to be tempted beyond our strength (1 Cor 10:13). We are weak, but God is strong. When we ask him for aid, he communicates his strength to us, and we are able to do all things, as Paul reasonably assured himself: "In him who is the source of my strength I have strength for everything" (Phil 4:13). The man who falls has no excuse if he has neglected to pray. For if he had prayed, he would not have been overcome by his enemies.

Is it necessary also to pray to the saints to obtain the grace of God? Not quite. But it is a lawful and useful thing to call on the saints as intercessors to obtain for us, by the merits of Jesus Christ, what we are not worthy to receive. This is a doctrine of the Church, declared by the Council of Trent.

It is lawful and profitable to ask living saints to assist us with their prayers, as God himself commanded the friends of Job to recommend themselves to his prayers, that by the merits of Job he might look favorably on them. If, then, it is lawful to recommend ourselves to the living, how can it be unlawful to invoke the saints who in heaven enjoy God face-to-face? This is not taking away the honor due to God, but doubling it, for it is honoring the King not only in his Person but in his servants.

Again, it is questioned whether there is any use in recommending oneself to the souls in purgatory. Some rely on the authority of St. Thomas who says that those souls "are not in a state to pray for us, but rather require our prayers." But many other Doctors, as, for example, St. Robert Bellarmine, affirm with great probability that we should believe God reveals our prayer to those holy souls so that they may pray for us. The souls in purgatory, being beloved of God and confirmed in grace, have absolutely no obstacle to prevent their praying for us. If we desire the help of their prayers, it is only fair that we should remember to help them with our prayers and good works. I said it is fair, but I should have said it is a Christian duty. For charity obliges us to help our neighbor when he requires our aid, and we can help him without excessive inconvenience. Now it is certain that among our neighbors are to be counted the souls in purgatory, who share in the communion of saints. They are destined to reign with Christ, but they are withheld from taking possession of their kingdom until the time of their purifying is accomplished.

On the other hand, since it is certain that by our sacrifices and our prayers we can relieve those holy souls, I do not know how to excuse that man who neglects to give them some assistance by his prayers. If a sense of duty will not persuade us to help them, let us think of the pleasure it will give Jesus Christ to see us trying to help them be with him in paradise. Let us think of the store of merits which we can gain by practicing this great act of charity. Those souls are not ungrateful and will never forget the great benefit we do them. And if God promises mercy to him who practices mercy toward his neighbor — "Blessed are they who show mercy; mercy shall be theirs" (Mt 5:7) — he may reasonably expect to be saved who remembers to assist those souls so dear to God.

If prayer to the saints and the souls in purgatory is so important, how much more so is prayer to our Blessed Lady. Mary's share in the work of salvation is unique. St. Bernard speaks to Mary: "Through you we have access to your Son, O discoverer of grace and Mother of salvation . . ." St. Bernard says in another place that Mary has received a twofold fullness of grace. The first was the Incarnation of the Word, who was made Man in her most holy womb. The second is that fullness of grace which we receive from God by means of her prayers. "God has placed the fullness of all good in Mary, that if we have any hope, any grace, any salvation, we may know that it overflows from her . . ." St. Augustine says that Mary is justly called our Mother because she cooperated by her charity in the birth of the faithful to the life of grace, by which we become members of Jesus Christ, our Head. Therefore, as Mary cooperated by her charity in the spiritual birth of the faithful, so also God willed that she should cooperate by her intercession to make them enjoy the life of grace in this world and the life of glory in the next. St. Bernard urges us to continually turn to the Mother of God because her prayers are certain to be heard by her Son: "Go to Mary, I say, without hesitation; the Son will hear the Mother."

At the conclusion of this first part, we stress again: Whoever prays is certainly saved. He who does not is certainly damned. All the blessed (except infants) have been saved by prayer. All the damned have been lost through not praying. If they had prayed, they would not have been lost. And this is, and will be, their greatest torment in hell: to think how easily they might have been saved, just by asking God for his grace, but that now it is too late — their time of prayer is gone.

B. Value of Prayer

In order to understand better the value of prayers in God's sight, it is enough to read the innumerable promises God makes to the man who prays, both in the Old and New Testaments. "Call to me, and I will answer you . . . " (Jer 33:3). "Then call upon me in time of distress; I will rescue you . . . " (Ps 50:15). "I give you my word, if you are ready to believe that you will receive whatever you ask for in prayer, it shall be done for you" (Mk 11:24). "I give you my assurance, whatever you ask the Father, he will give you in my name" (Jn 16:23). There are many similar texts, but it would take too long to quote them.

God wills us to be saved. But for our greater good, he wills us to be saved as conquerors. While we remain here we have to live in continual warfare, and if we are to be saved we have to fight and conquer. "No one can be crowned without victory," says St. John Chrysostom. We are very weak and our enemies are many and mighty. How shall we be able to stand against them or to defeat them? Let us take courage and say with St. Paul, "In him who is the source of my strength I have strength for everything" (Phil 4:13).

God knows the great good it does us to need to pray, and he permits us to be assaulted by our enemies in order that we may ask him for the help which he offers and promises to us. He is pleased when we run to him in our dangers; he is displeased when he sees us neglectful of prayer. As the king, says St. Bonaventure, would consider an officer unfaithful who did not ask him for reinforcements when his post was attacked, so God thinks himself betrayed by the man who is surrounded by temptations and does not run to him for assistance. For he desires to help us; he only waits to be asked, and then gives abundant help. This is strikingly shown by Isaiah when, on God's behalf, he told King Ahaz to ask for some sign to prove to himself God's readiness to help him: "Ask for a sign from the Lord, your God" (Is 7:11). The faithless king answered: "I will not ask! I will not tempt the Lord," for he trusted in his own power to overcome his enemies without God's aid. And for this the prophet admonished him. For that man is offensive to God who will not ask him for the graces which he offers.

If God were to allow us to present our petitions to him once a month, even this would be a great favor. The kings of the earth give audiences a few times a year, but God gives a continual audience. St. John Chrysostom writes that God is always waiting to hear our prayers, and that a case never occurred when he neglected to hear a petition offered to him properly. And in another place he says that when we pray to God, before we have finished telling him our requests, he has already heard us. We even have the promise of God to do this:

"While they are yet speaking, I will hearken to them" (Is 65:24).

We are so poor that we have nothing. But if we pray, we are no longer poor. If we are poor, God is rich. Since we have a Lord of infinite power and infinite riches, let us not go to him for little valueless things, but let us ask some great thing of him: "You seek from the Almighty — seek something great." "You may ask what you will — it will be done for you" (Jn 15:7).

On this point, then, we have to fix all our attention, namely, to pray with confidence, feeling sure that by prayer all the treasures of heaven are thrown open to us. "Let us attend to this," says St. John Chrysostom, "and we shall open heaven to ourselves." Prayer is a treasure; he who prays most receives most. St. Bonaventure says that every time a man turns to God by fervent prayer, he gains good things that are of more value than the whole world. There is no doubt that spiritual reading and meditation on the eternal truths are very useful things; but, says St. Augustine, it is of much more use to pray." By reading and meditation we learn our duty, but by prayer we obtain the grace to do it: "It is better to pray than to read: by reading we know what we ought to do; by prayer we receive what we ask." We shall never satisfy our obligations unless we ask of God the grace to fulfill them.

The devil is never busier trying to distract us than when he sees us praying and asking God for grace. And why? Because the enemy sees that at no other time do we gain so many treasures of heavenly goods as when we pray. This is the chief benefit of prayer, to ask God for the graces we need for perseverance and eternal salvation. A person who prays thoughtfully every day will easily see the needs of his soul, its dangers, and the necessity of his prayer, and so he will pray and will obtain the graces which will enable him to persevere and save his soul.

We ought to pray as soon as we wake up in the morning, and then continue doing it in all our needs and in setting about all our business, and most especially when we find ourselves troubled by any temptation or passion. St. Bonaventure says that at times we obtain a grace sooner by a short prayer than by many other good works. St. John Chrysostom wrote that, "There is nothing more powerful than a man who prays," because such a one is made partaker of the power of God. To arrive at perfection, said St. Bernard, we must meditate and pray. By meditation we see what we want; by prayer we receive what we want. "The one teaches what is lacking, the other assures that there should be nothing lacking."

To save one's soul without prayer is most difficult, and perhaps even impossible, according to the ordinary course of God's providence. But by praying our salvation is made secure and very easy. It is not necessary for salvation to go to foreign missions and give up our life. It is not necessary to become a hermit and fast for long periods. What does it cost us to say, My God, help me! Lord, assist me! Have mercy on me! Is there anything easier than this? These few words are enough to save us if we will be faithful in saying them. Let no one, says St. Bernard, think lightly of prayer, because God values it; and then he gives us either what we ask or what is even more useful to us. And let us understand that if we do not pray we have no excuse, because the grace of prayer is given to everyone. It is in our power to pray whenever we will to do so.

C. Conditions of Prayer

"I give you my assurance, whatever you ask the Father, he will give you in my name" (Jn 16:23). Jesus Christ has promised that whatever we ask his Father in his name, his Father will give us. But he does so, always with the understanding that we ask under the proper conditions. Many seek, says St. James, but do not obtain because they seek improperly: "You ask and you do not receive because you ask wrongly" (Jas 4:3). So St. Basil, following out the argument of the apostle, says, "You sometimes ask and fail to receive because you have asked badly, either faithlessly or lightly; or you have requested things not fit for you, or you have not persevered." "Faithlessly," that is, with little faith or confidence. "Lightly," with little desire for the grace you request. "Things not fit for you," when you seek good things that will not be helpful to your salvation. Or you have left off praying and have lost "perseverance." St. Thomas reduces to four the conditions required in prayer in order that it may procure its effect. These are that a man ask: 1) *for himself*; 2) *things necessary for salvation*; 3) *devoutly*; and 4) *with perseverance*.

When a man prays for his own needs, he naturally thinks of the needs of others. No soul that really loves God neglects to pray for poor sinners. For how is it possible for a person who loves God, and knows what love he has for our souls and what Jesus Christ has done and suffered for their salvation, to look with indifference on the numbers of poor souls who are living without God? God, with the help of our prayers, often sees fit to bring back the most blinded and stubborn sinners to a state of salvation by means of extraordinary graces. Therefore we should never fail to recommend poor sinners to God. A learned author says that he who prays for others will find that his prayers for himself are heard much sooner.

A man may pray faithfully for the necessities of this life, and God may mercifully refuse to hear him, because the physician knows better than the patient what is good for the sick man. When men ask God for health or riches, he often denies them because he loves them, knowing that these things would be an occasion of losing his grace, or at any rate of growing weak in the spiritual life. We do not mean to say that it is wrong to pray to God for the needs of this present life, so far as they are not inconsistent with our eternal salvation. Nor is it a defect, says St. Thomas, to have anxiety about such goods, if it is not overdone. The defect consists in desiring and seeking these material goods and in having an excessive anxiety about them, as if they were our highest good. Therefore, when we ask God for these material favors, we ought always to ask for them with the condition that they will be useful to our souls. When we see that God does not grant them, let us be certain that he then denies them to us because of the love he bears us, and because he sees that they would be harmful to the salvation of our souls.

It often happens that we pray to God to deliver us from some dangerous temptation, and yet God does not hear us, but permits the temptation to continue troubling us. In such a case, we should understand that God permits even this for our greater good. It is not temptation or bad thoughts that separate us from God, but our consent to the evil. When a soul in temptation turns to God and by his help resists, that soul then advances in perfection, and is united more closely to God! We ought to pray in temptations, saying: Lord, deliver me from this trouble, if it is truly good to deliver me; and if not, at least give me help to resist. Be sure that God, then, really hears us and is secretly aiding us and strengthening us by his grace to resist all the assaults of our enemies. He himself assures us of this by the mouth of King David: "In distress you called, and I rescued you . . . " (Ps 81:8).

(Here we will treat the above conditions under three headings. We must pray with humility, with confidence, and with perseverance.)

1) Prayer Demands Humility

We all ought to realize that we are supported only by the power of God's grace. If this power fails us, we shall certainly fall: "Were not the Lord my help, I would soon dwell in the silent grave" (Ps 94:17). We must believe that without the aid of grace we cannot do any good work nor even think a good thought. As the eye cannot see without light, so, said St. Augustine, man can do no good without grace. St. Paul had said the same thing before him: "It is not that we are entitled of ourselves to take credit for anything. Our sole credit is from God . . . " (2 Cor 3:5). And David had said it before St. Paul: "Unless the Lord build the house, they labor in vain who build it" (Ps 127:1). In vain does man weary himself to become a saint, unless God lends a helping hand: "Unless the Lord guard the city, in vain does the guard keep vigil" (Ps 127:1). If God did not preserve the soul from sins, in vain would she try to preserve herself by her own strength.

If a man says he has no fear, it is a sign that he trusts in himself and in his good resolutions. But such a man deceives himself, because through trust in his own strength he neglects to fear, and through not fearing he neglects to recommend himself to God, and then he certainly will fall. We should all stop scowling at the sins of other people. Rather, we should consider that we may be worse spiritually than they are and should say, "Lord, if you had not helped me, I should have done worse." Otherwise, to punish us for our pride, God will permit us to fall into worse and more shameful sins. For this reason St. Paul instructs us to work for our salvation. But how? Always in fear and trembling (Phil 2:12). The man who has a great fear of falling distrusts his own strength and therefore places his confidence in God and will turn to him in dangers. God will then aid him so that he will defeat his temptations and be saved.

And so, with the help of God, who never refuses anything to the man who prays to him with humility, he will be able to do all things: "The prayer of the lowly pierces the clouds; it does not rest till it reaches its goal, nor will it withdraw till the Most High responds" (Sir 35:17-18).

2) Prayer Demands Confidence

When did it ever happen that a man had

confidence in God and was lost? Says St. Augustine: "God is not a deceiver, that he should offer to support us, and then when we lean upon him should slip away from us." David calls the man happy who trusts in God: "O Lord of hosts, happy the men who trust in you!" (Ps 84:13) And why? Because he who trusts in God will always find himself surrounded by God's mercy so that he will be guarded by God on every side and be prevented from losing his soul.

David said that our confidence in God ought to be firm as a mountain, which is not moved by each gust of wind: "They who trust in the Lord are like Mount Zion, which is immovable . . . " (Ps 125:1). It is this which our Lord recommends to us if we wish to obtain the graces which we ask: "If you are ready to believe . . . it shall be done for you" (Mk 11:24).

But what is the basis of this certain confidence of obtaining what I ask? It is the promise made by Jesus Christ, "Ask and you shall receive" (Jn 16:24). "Who will fear to be deceived, when the truth promises?" says St. Augustine. How can we doubt our being heard when God, who is truth itself, promises to give us what we ask of him in prayer? Pray, ask, seek, and you will obtain what you desire. Our Savior has taught us in the "Our Father" that we should call him not Lord but Father — "Our Father" — because it is his will that we should ask God for grace with the same confidence with which a son, when in need or in sickness, asks food or medicine from his own father.

Trusting in God's promises, let us always pray with confidence, not wavering, but stable and firm: "Let us hold unswervingly to our profession which gives us hope, for he who made the promise deserves our trust" (Heb 10:23). As it is certain that God is faithful in his promises, so our faith should be certain that he will hear us when we pray. Sometimes, when we feel spiritually dried up or disturbed by some fault we have committed, we perhaps do not feel that prayerful confidence which we would wish to experience. In spite of this, let us force ourselves to pray and to pray without ceasing, for God will not neglect to hear us. No, on the contrary, he will hear us more readily, because we shall then pray with more distrust of ourselves and with more trust in God who has promised to hear the man who prays to him.

If we have great confidence when we pray, we shall get what we want from God. The Canaanite woman did so, and she obtained all she wished from Jesus Christ. This woman had a daughter possessed by a devil, and prayed that Jesus would free her: "Lord, Son of David, have pity on me! My daughter is terribly troubled by a demon" (Mt 15:22). Our Lord answered that he had been sent first of all to aid his own people, not the gentiles. However she did not lose heart, but renewed her prayer with confidence: "Help me, Lord!" Jesus replied, "It is not right to take the food of sons and daughters and throw it to the dogs." But, my Lord, she answered, even the dogs are allowed to have the fragments of bread which fall from the table. Then our Savior, seeing the great confidence of this woman, praised her and did what she asked, saying, "Woman, you have great faith! Your wish will come to pass." For who, says the author of Sirach, has ever called on God for aid and has been neglected and left unaided by him? (2:10)

When we find ourselves weak and unable to overcome any passion or any great difficulty to fulfill what God requires of us, we should take courage and not say, as some do: I cannot, I distrust myself. With our own strength certainly we can do nothing, but with God's help we can do everything. Let us pray with David: "The Lord is with me; I fear not; what can man do against me?" (Ps 118:6) With the help of my Lord, I shall overcome. And when we find ourselves in danger of offending God, or in any other critical position, and are too confused to know what is best to do, let us recommend ourselves to God, saying, "The Lord is my light and my salvation; whom should I fear?" (Ps 27:1) We can be sure then that God will certainly give us light and will save us from every evil.

We read in John's Gospel the words of the blind man who was cured: "We know that God does not hear sinners, but that if someone is devout and obeys his will, he listens to him" (Jn 9:31). God does not hear the petition which the sinner makes when he asks while at the same time desiring to continue in sin. The same is true for the sinner who prays God to save him, but has no desire to quit the state of sin. The prayers of such men are not heard by God.

Persons who sin due to weakness, or by the violence of some great passion, but who really desire to escape from slavery to sin should ask the assistance of God. Their prayer, if it is persevering, will certainly be heard by him. In St. Luke's Gospel, Jesus, speaking of the man who gave all the loaves he had to his friend, not so much because of his friendship as because of the other's strong request, says, "I tell you, even though he does not get up and take care of the man because of friendship, he will do so because of his persistence, and give him as much as he needs. So I say to you, 'Ask and you shall receive . . . ' " (Lk 11:8-9). Continued prayer obtains mercy from God, even for those who are not in his grace. St. Jerome says that even the sinner can call God his Father if he prays him to be accepted again as a son. The prodigal son returned to say: "Father, I have sinned," even though he had not as yet been pardoned. If God did not hear sinners, says St. Augustine, it would have been useless for the tax collector to seek forgiveness. But the Gospel assures us that the tax collector prayed and did obtain forgiveness: "This man went home from the temple justified"

(Lk 18:14).

St. John Chrysostom says that the only time God is angry with us is when we neglect to ask him for his gifts: "He is only angry when we do not pray." And how can it ever happen that God will not hear a soul who asks him for favors all according to his pleasure? When the soul says to him, Lord, I do not ask you for goods of this world, riches, pleasures, honors; I ask you only for your grace: deliver me from sin, grant me a good death, give me paradise, give me your love, help me to accept your will — how is it possible that God should not hear? Above all, our confidence ought to revive when we pray to God for spiritual graces, as Jesus Christ says, "If you, with all your sins, know how to give your children good things, how much more will the heavenly Father give the Holy Spirit to those who ask him!" (Lk 11:13) If you, who are so attached to your own interests, so full of self-love, cannot deny your children what they ask, how much more will your heavenly Father, who loves you better than any earthly father, grant you his spiritual goods when you pray for them!

3) Prayer Demands Perseverance

Our prayers, then, must be humble and confident. But this is not enough to obtain final perseverance for eternal life. Individual prayers will obtain individual graces from God, but the grace of final perseverance requires many prayers, right up until death. The grace of salvation is not a single grace, but a chain of graces, all of which are at last linked with the grace of final perseverance. Now to this chain of graces there ought to correspond another chain of our prayers. If we, by neglecting to pray, break the chain of our prayers, the chain of graces will be broken too, and we shall not be saved. "So be on the watch. Pray constantly for the strength to escape whatever is in prospect, and to stand secure before the Son of Man" (Lk 21:36).

Since God can give me the grace of perseverance, and really wishes to, why does he not give it to me all at once when I ask him? God does not grant it at once, but delays it, first, so that he may better prove our confidence and, secondly, so that we may long for it more forcefully. Great gifts should be greatly desired, for good things easily gotten are not valued as much as those which have been long sought for. If we were already sure of persevering and of being saved, and if we did not have continual need of God's help to preserve us in his grace and to save us, we should soon forget God. God wishes to make us careful and to draw us to himself. Our continual turning to God in prayer and the confident expectation of the graces which we desire from him stimulate and inflame us to bind ourselves more closely to God!

But for how long must we pray? Always until we receive favorable sentence of eternal life, that is to say, until our death. The man who will never stop praying until he is saved will most certainly be saved. St. Paul writes that many run for the prize, but that he only receives it who runs until he wins (1 Cor 9:24). It is not enough for salvation simply to pray, but we must pray always in order to receive the crown which God promises, but promises only to those who are constant in prayer to the end.

II

EVERYBODY GETS THE
GRACE TO PRAY

Taking for granted, then, that prayer is necessary for gaining eternal life, we should also take for granted that everyone has sufficient aid from God to enable him to pray. By prayer he may obtain all other graces necessary to persevere in keeping the commandments and so gain eternal life. No one who is lost can ever excuse himself by saying that it was through lack of the aid necessary for his salvation. God in the natural order arranged that man should be born naked and lacking several things necessary for life, but then has given him hands and intelligence to clothe himself and provide for his other needs. In the supernatural order man is born unable to obtain salvation by his own strength, but God in his goodness grants to everyone the grace of prayer by which he can gain all other graces which he needs to keep the commandments and be saved.

Before expanding this theme, we will consider two preliminary points: first, that God wills all men to be saved and, therefore, that Jesus Christ died for all; secondly, that God gives to all men the graces necessary for salvation, by which they may be saved if they cooperate with them.

A. God Wills All Men to Be Saved

God loves all things that he has created: "For you love all things that are and loathe nothing that you have made" (Wis 11:24). The person who loves cannot help doing good to the person beloved whenever there is an opportunity: "Love persuades a man to do what he believes to be good for the one he loves," says Aristotle. If God loves all men, he must then will that all men reach eternal salvation, which is the greatest good of man, the one end for which he was created. God "wants all men to be saved and come to know the truth" (1 Tm 2:4). Therefore, the grace of God is lacking to no man; he makes it available to everyone.

If God punishes us, he does it because of our sins. He does not will our death, but our life. It is God's proper nature to save all, and to deliver all from eternal death. St. Peter says: "He wants none to perish but all to come to repentance" (2 Pt 3:9). He does not will the damnation of anyone, but he wills that all should do penance and so should be saved.

All the holy Fathers agree in saying that Jesus Christ died to obtain eternal salvation for all men. St. Jerome: "Christ died for all; he was the only one who could be offered for all, because all were dead in sins." St. Ambrose: "Christ came to cure our wounds; but since all do not search for the remedy . . . therefore he cures those who are willing; he does not force the unwilling." God, for his part, really wills us all to be saved; otherwise, it would not be in our power to obtain health and eternal life. He who redeemed us at such a cost does not will that we perish, for he does not purchase in order to destroy, but he redeems in order to give life. He has redeemed us all in order to save us all. We are encouraged to hope for eternal happiness by what Christ has done and has promised. What has he done? He has died for us. What has he promised? That we shall live with him.

St. Augustine left no doubt when he said, "All my hope, and the certainty of my faith, is in the precious blood of Christ, which was shed for us and for our salvation." Thus the saint placed all his hope in the blood of Jesus Christ, because the faith assured him that Christ died for all.

B. This Means Both the Just and Sinners

If God wills all to be saved, it follows that he gives to all that grace and those aids which are necessary for salvation. Otherwise, it could never be said that he has a true will to save all. God does not impose a law that it is impossible to observe. On the other hand, it is certain that without the assistance of grace the observance of the law is impossible. If God refused us grace to enable us to fulfill the law, either the law would have been given in vain, or sin would be necessary, and if necessary would no longer be sin.

As the sun sheds its light upon all, and only those are deprived of it who voluntarily blind themselves to its rays, so God communicates to all men grace to observe the law, and men are lost simply because they will not make use of it. God gives all men the graces necessary for salvation. Actual grace is necessary to overcome temptations and to observe the commandments. We must necessarily conclude that he gives all men the actual grace to do good.

Scripture, in several places, most clearly assures us that he does not neglect to assist us with his grace if we are willing to make use of it, either for perseverance if we are in a state of grace, or for conversion if we are in sin. "Here I stand, knocking at the door. If anyone hears me calling and opens the door, I will enter his house ... "

(Rv 3:20). Our Lord knows that man cannot open without his grace.

This is exactly what St. Thomas teaches in explaining the text. He says that God gives everyone the grace necessary for salvation, so that he may cooperate with it if he wishes. "God by his most liberal will gives grace to everyone who prepares himself." Therefore, the grace of God is lacking to no one, but communicates itself to all men. In another place he says, "It is the business of God's providence to provide everyone with what is necessary to salvation." The Lord knocks at the gate because he truly wishes to enter; if he does not enter or if he does not remain in our souls, it is because we prevent his entering or drive him out when he has entered.

"Do you not know that God's kindness is an invitation to you to repent?" (Rom 2:4) It is through his own malice that the sinner is not converted, because he despises the riches of God's goodness which calls him untiringly to conversion by grace. God hates sin, but at the same time never stops loving the sinful soul while it remains on earth, and always gives it the assistance it requires for salvation: "But you spare all things, because they are yours, O Lord and lover of souls" (Wis 11:26).

St. Robert Bellarmine writes: "Assistance to avoid new sin is always at hand for all men, either immediately or mediately" (that is, by means of prayer), "so that they may ask further aid from God to avoid sin." In the Book of Ezekiel we read: "As I live, says the Lord God, I swear I take no pleasure in the death of the wicked man, but rather in the wicked man's conversion, that he may live" (Ez 33:11). St. Peter says the same, "The Lord . . . shows you generous patience, since he wants none to perish but all to come to repentance" (2 Pt 3:9). If, therefore, God wishes that all should actually be converted, it must necessarily be held that he gives to all the grace they need for actual conversion.

St. Paul teaches: "God keeps his promise. He will not let you be tested beyond your strength. Along with the test he will give you a way out of it so that you may be able to endure it" (1 Cor 10:13). And Saints Augustine and Thomas go so far as to say that God would be unjust and cruel if he obliged anyone to a command which he could not keep. The former says, "It is the deepest injustice to judge anyone guilty of sin for not doing what he could not do." The latter maintains that it is considered cruelty in a man to oblige a person by law to do what he cannot do; therefore, we must by no means imagine this of God. But he adds that the case is different "when it is through his own neglect that man does not have the grace to be able to keep the commandments." And the Council of Trent teaches, "God does not command impossibilities, but by commanding, urges you both to do what you can and to ask for what is beyond your power, and by his help he enables you to do it."

C. Man Makes the Choice

Assuming, then, that God wills all men to be saved, and that as far as he is concerned he gives to all the graces necessary for their salvation, we must say that all men are given the grace to enable them to pray and, by prayer, to obtain all further aid needed for observing the commandments and for salvation.

No Father is clearer on this point than St. Augustine. According to him, no one is deprived of the grace of prayer to obtain help for his conversion. Otherwise, if this grace were lacking, it could not be his fault if he were not converted. "It is he who gives us power to ask and to seek and to knock who commands us to do these things . . . He gives us commandments for this reason: that when we have tried to do what we are commanded and are wearied through our weakness, we may know how to ask the help of grace."

In making this choice, we call on the virtue of hope which is so pleasing to God that he has said he delights in those who trust in him: "The Lord is pleased with those who . . . hope for his kindness" (Ps 147:11). And he promises victory over his enemies, perseverance in grace, and eternal glory to the man who hopes. "Has anyone hoped in the Lord and been disappointed?" (Sir 2:10) We can be sure that, though heaven and earth pass away, the promises of God cannot fail: "The heavens and the earth will pass away but my words will not pass" (Mt 24:35). St. Bernard, therefore, says that all our merit consists in placing all our confidence in God: "This is the whole merit of man, if he places all his hope in him." The reason is that he who hopes in God honors him much: "Then call upon me in time of distress; I will rescue you, and you shall glorify me" (Ps 50:15). He honors the power, the mercy, and the faithfulness of God, since he believes that God can and will save him, and that he cannot fail in his promises to save the man who trusts in him. The greater our confidence is, the greater will be the measure of God's mercy poured out upon us: "May your kindness, O Lord, be upon us who have put our hope in you" (Ps 33:22). Hope of eternal life ought to be sure and firm in us.

The Council of Trent has expressly declared, "All men should place and keep a most firm hope in the help of God; for, unless they fail to cooperate with his grace, he who has begun the good work will finish it . . ." And long before, St. Paul had said of himself, "I know him in whom I have believed, and I am confident that he is able to guard what has been entrusted to me until that Day" (2 Tm 1:12). Herein lies the difference between Christian and worldly hope. Worldly hope is often just an uncertain expectation.

It is always doubtful whether or not a

man who has promised a favor may later change his mind, if he has not already changed it. But the Christian hope of eternal salvation is certain on God's part, for he can and will save us and has promised to save those who obey his law. For this reason he has promised us all necessary graces to enable us to obey this law, if we ask for them. It is true that hope is accompanied by fear, as St. Thomas says; but this fear does not arise from God's part but from our own, since we may at any time fail by not cooperating as we should and by putting an obstacle in the way of grace by our sins. Reasonably, then, did the Council of Trent condemn those who, because they entirely deprive man of free will, are obliged to make every believer have an infallible certitude of perseverance and salvation. This error was condemned by the Council because, as we have said, in order to obtain salvation it is necessary for us to cooperate, and this cooperation of ours is uncertain and fallible. Therefore, God wills that we should always fear for ourselves when we presume on our own strength; but we should be always certain of his good will and of his assistance to save us, provided that we ask him for it. St. Thomas says we ought to look with certainty to receive eternal happiness from God, trusting in his power and mercy and believing that he can and will save us. "Whoever has faith is certain of God's power and mercy."

This is why the apostle James declares

that the man who desires God's grace must ask for it, not with hesitation but with the confident certainty of obtaining it. "Yet he must ask in faith, never doubting" (Jas 1:6). And St. Paul praises Abraham for not doubting God's promise; Abraham knew that when God promises, he cannot fail to perform: "Yet he never questioned or doubted God's promise; rather, he was strengthened in faith and gave glory to God, fully persuaded that God could do whatever he had promised" (Rom 4:20-21).

To sum up: Our hope of salvation and of receiving the means necessary for it must be certain on God's part. The motives on which this certainty is founded are the power, mercy, and truth of God. The strongest and most certain motive is God's infallible faithfulness to the promise he has made us through the merits of Jesus Christ, to save us and to give us the graces needed for our salvation. We might believe God to be infinite in power and mercy; nevertheless, we could not feel confident expectation of God's saving us unless he had surely promised to do so. He has made that promise, but there is a condition: We must actively cooperate with God's grace and pray.

We have seen that many passages both of the Old and New Testament show the absolute necessity of prayer. This is why a sermon on prayer is preached on all the missions given by our Redemptorists. I say and repeat, and will keep repeating as long as I live, that all our salvation depends on prayer.

All writers in their books, all preachers in their sermons, all confessors in their instructions to their penitents should not urge anything more strongly than continual prayer. They should always encourage and continually repeat: Pray, pray, never cease to pray. For if you pray, your salvation will be assured; but if you stop praying, your damnation will be certain. All preachers and directors ought to do this because, according to the opinion of every Catholic school of theology, there is no doubt of this truth: He who prays obtains grace and is saved.

love of god

and

how to gain it

I
GOD LOVES YOU. DO YOU LOVE HIM?

Our Lord, because he loves us much, desires to be much loved by us. Therefore, he has not only called us to love him by many invitations often repeated in Scripture, but he also obliges us to love him by an explicit commandment. He threatens with hell those who do not love him, while to those who do love him he promises paradise. His will is that no one be lost, but that all attain salvation, as St. Peter and St. Paul most clearly teach: "He wants all men to be saved" (1 Tm 2:4). "The Lord . . . shows you generous patience, since he wants none to perish but all to come to repentance" (2 Pt 3:9). But since God wishes all men to be saved, why has he created hell? He did so, not to see us damned, but in order to be loved by us. If he had not created hell, who in the whole world would love him? If, with hell existing, many men choose to be damned rather than to love almighty God, who, I repeat, would love him if there were no hell? And therefore the Lord threatens those who will not love him with eternal punishment, so that they who will not love him out of love may at least love him through fear of falling into hell.

O God, how fortunate and honored would that man be to whom his king should say, "Love me because I love you!" An earthly monarch would take good care not to humble himself to such an extent as to ask one of his subjects for his love. But God, who is infinite goodness, the Lord of all, almighty, all-wise, who merits an infinite love, who has enriched us with spiritual and temporal gifts, does not shrink from asking for our love. He exhorts and commands us to love him, but many refuse to respond. What does he ask each one of us but to be loved? "What does the Lord, your God, ask of you but to fear the Lord, your God, . . . to love and serve [him]?" (Dt 10:12) It was for this reason that the Son of God came to earth, as he himself said: "I am come to light a fire on the earth. How I wish the blaze were ignited!" (Lk 12:49) Notice those last words — "How I wish the blaze were ignited!" It is as if God, who possesses in himself infinite happiness, could not be happy without seeing himself loved by us: "As if," says St. Thomas, "he could not be happy without you."

We cannot doubt, then, that God loves us, and loves us greatly. Because he loves us greatly, he wishes us to love him with our whole heart: "You shall love the Lord, your God, with all your heart." And then he adds: "Take to heart these words which I enjoin on you today. Drill them into your children. Speak of them at home and abroad, whether you are busy or at rest. Bind them at your wrist as a sign and let them be as a pendant on your forehead. Write them on the doorposts of your houses and on your gates" (Dt 6:5-9). We can see in all these words how earnestly God desires to be loved by each one of us. He wishes that the injunction of loving him with our whole heart should be imprinted in our heart, and that we never forget these words. He wishes us to meditate upon them when we are sitting at home, when we are walking abroad, when we lie down to sleep, and when we wake from it again. He wishes us to hold them in our hands bound up with some significant memento in order that, wherever we may be, our eyes may always rest upon them. Thus the Pharisees, taking the words only in their literal sense, as we are told by St. Matthew, used to wear them inscribed on broad pieces of parchment which hung on their foreheads (Mt 23:5).

St. Gregory of Nyssa exclaims, "Blessed

is the arrow which carries along with it into the heart the God by whom it is aimed!" What the holy Father means is this: When God wounds the heart with an arrow of love, it acts like a flash or ray of special illumination, whereby the soul becomes aware of his goodness and of the love which he bears toward her, and also of the desire which he has to possess the love of that soul; at the same time he himself comes together with that arrow of his love. And as an arrow remains fixed in the heart which it has wounded, so in the same way does God, when he wounds a soul with his love, come to remain forever united with that soul which he has wounded. Let us be assured that it is God only who loves us truly. The love of parents, of friends, and of all others who say they love us (except those who love us solely out of regard for God) is not a true but a self-interested love, and arises from some motive of self-love for the sake of which we are loved.

My God, I know full well that it is you alone who loves me, and desires for me every good, not for any selfish interests of your own, but solely out of your own goodness and out of the pure affection which you have for me, while I am so ungrateful as to have caused no one so much displeasure and so many griefs as I have done to you. Jesus, do not permit me to be ungrateful to you any more. You have loved me truly, and I wish to love you truly in whatever of this life may still be mine. With St. Catherine of Genoa, I say to you: "My Love, no more sins, no more sins." I wish to love you only, and nothing else.

St. Bernard says that a soul which truly loves God "cannot will anything but what God wills." Let us pray God to wound us with his holy love, for a soul thus wounded has neither the faculty nor the power to have a will for anything but that which God wills; it divests itself of every desire arising out of self-love.

How beautifully St. Bernard expresses himself on this subject when he says: "Let us learn to dart our hearts at God!" When a soul gives herself up wholly and unreservedly to God, it is as if she darted her own heart like a spear toward the heart of God, who declares himself to be, as it were, captured and taken prisoner by such a soul. This is the employment of such souls in the prayers which they offer: "They dart their hearts at God"; they give themselves wholly up to God, and they are ever renewing that gift in these or similar thoughts of love:

My God and my all: My God, I long for you and for nothing else.

O Lord, I give myself wholly to you, and if I do not know how to make the gift as perfect as I ought, do it yourself.

And what would I love, my Jesus, if I do not love you who have died for me?

Since you have called me to your love, enable me to please you as you desire.

And what would I love but you who are infinite goodness, deserving infinite love?

You have inspired me with the desire of being entirely yours; make the work complete!

And what would I have in this world but you, who are the sovereign Good?

I give myself to you without reserve; accept me, and give me the strength to be faithful till death!

I wish to love you greatly in this life, that I may love you greatly for all eternity.

II

FIVE WAYS TO GOD'S LOVE

Blessed, in short, is that soul which can truly say, "My lover belongs to me and I to him" (Song 2:16). My God has given himself entirely to me, and I have given myself entirely to him. I am no longer my own; I belong entirely to my God. St. Bernard says that whoever can say this from his heart would most readily and willingly embrace all the pains of hell (provided that he could do so without separating himself from God) rather than see himself, even for one single moment, disunited from God:

"It would be more tolerable to such a one to suffer hell than to withdraw from him." What a beautiful treasure is the treasure of divine love! He who possesses it is happy indeed. Let him take every care, and make use of all the means which are necessary to preserve and increase it. He who does not yet possess it ought to use every means in order to acquire it. Here are five ways, or means, to gain God's love.

A. Detachment from Worldly Affections

The *first* of these means is the detachment of oneself from worldly affections. In a heart which is full of the world, no room can be found for the love of God. The more the worldly element predominates, so much the less does the divine love hold sway. Therefore, he who desires to have his heart filled with divine love should remove from it all that is of the world. To become saints we must follow the example of St. Paul who, so that he might gain the love of Jesus Christ, despised as nothing all the good things of this world (Phil 3:8). Let us pray the Holy Spirit to enkindle within us his holy love, for then we too shall despise and reckon as mere vanity all this world's riches, pleasures, honors, and distinctions, for the sake of which men suffer eternal destruction.

Whenever holy love enters into the heart, it no longer regards as of any value all that the world holds dear. St. Francis de Sales observes that when a house is in flames the goods are all thrown out through the windows, meaning that when the heart is on fire with divine love a man does not need the preachings and exhortations of a spiritual father, but of his own accord sets to work to divest himself of the good things of this world in order that he may love nothing but God. St. Catherine of Genoa used to say that she did not love God for the sake of his gifts, but that she loved the gifts of God so that she might love him the more.

How hard it is for the lover to divide his heart between Christ and the world! St. Bernard says that the divine love is, on the other hand, exclusive, because God will not permit that, in a heart which loves, there should be others to share with him in its love. Does God claim too much in wishing that a soul should love him, and him alone? "The sovereign Loveliness," observes St. Bonaventure, "ought to be loved exclusively." Such a one as God, whose loveliness and goodness are infinite and worthy of an infinite love, has a just claim to be alone in his possession of the love of a heart created by himself. In order that he might be loved exclusively, he has gone so far as to expend himself wholly for that heart. As St. Bernard says when speaking of himself and of the love which Jesus Christ had borne toward him: "He was utterly spent for my benefit." What each one of us can most truly say when thinking of Jesus Christ is that for each one of us he has sacrificed all his life and all his blood, dying upon a Cross. And, although his death is past, he has left us his body and his blood, his soul and his whole self in the sacrament of the altar, that it may be the meat and drink of our souls and that we may each be united to him.

Happy is the soul which has arrived at a state wherein everything is intolerable except the God whom it loves. We must, then, be on our guard against setting our affections on creatures, lest they steal from us a portion of the love which God wishes to be entirely his own. Even when such affections are right, as in the case of those we feel toward parents or friends, we should never forget the saying of St. Philip Neri, that whatever love we have for creatures is so much taken away from God.

We should, therefore, try to make ourselves "enclosed gardens," as the bride in the Song of Songs was called by her lover. The title of "an enclosed garden" applies to that soul which keeps itself closed up against the entrance of all mere earthly affections. Whenever, therefore, any creature seeks to enter in and to lay hold of a portion of our heart, we must refuse it admission. Then we ought to turn to Jesus Christ and say to him: My Jesus, you alone are sufficient for me. I do not wish to love anyone but you. You are the God of my heart, and the God that is my portion forever. On this account, let us not cease praying to God that he would bestow upon us the gift of his pure love since, as St. Francis de Sales observes, "The pure love of God consumes all that is not God, to transform everything into itself."

B. Meditation on the Passion of Christ

Meditation on the Passion of our Lord Jesus Christ is the *second* means for acquiring divine love. It is certain that Jesus Christ is so little loved in the world because of the negligence and ingratitude of mankind, and because men do not consider, at least occasionally, how much he has suffered for us. "To mankind it has appeared foolish," as St. Gregory observes, "that God should die for us." It seems folly, says the saint, that God should have been willing to die in order to save us; yet he did so. He has loved us, and delivered himself for us. And he has shed all his blood in order to wash away our sins.

St. Bonaventure says, "My God, you have loved me so much that you seem to have gone so far as even to have hated yourself." Besides, he has willed that he himself should be our food in Holy Communion. St. Thomas, speaking of the Blessed Sacrament, says that God has so humbled himself with us that it is as if he were our servant, and each of us his God.

"The love of Christ impels us" (2 Cor 5:14). St. Paul says that the love which Jesus Christ has borne us forces us, in a certain sense, to love him. My God, what is there that men will not do out of love for some creature on which they have set their affections! And how little is their love for one who is God, whose goodness and loveliness are infinite, and who has even gone so far as to die on a Cross for each of us! Let us follow the example of St. Paul who said: "May I never boast of anything but the cross of our Lord Jesus Christ" (Gal 6:14). So spoke the holy apostle, and what greater glory can I hope for in the world than that of having had a God to sacrifice his life for me? This is what everyone who has faith must say; if he has faith, how can it be possible for him to love anything other than God? How can a soul, contemplating Jesus crucified, as he hangs suspended on three nails, and dies because of his love for us, not see itself drawn and, as it were, forced to love him with all its powers?

C. Conformity to God's Will

The *third* means of gaining a perfect love of God is the bringing of our own will into conformity with the divine will in all things. St. Bernard says that he who loves God perfectly "cannot will anything except that which God wills." There are many who profess themselves to be thoroughly resigned to whatever God wills, but when any adverse circumstance or any sickness befalls them, they cannot retain their peace of mind. It is not so with souls in a state of true conformity. They say, "Thus it pleases him whom I love," and they are immediately at rest. "To holy love," says St. Bonaventure, "all things are sweet." These souls know that everything which happens in the world is either ordered or permitted by God. Consequently, in all that comes to pass, they humbly bow their heads and live contented with what God assigns. Although it is frequently the case that he does not will that those who persecute and injure us should do so, yet he nevertheless wills, and for wise ends, that we should suffer with patience the persecution or the injury by which we are afflicted.

St. Catherine of Genoa used to say, "If God had placed me in the depths of hell, I would sincerely have said, it is good for us to be here." I would have said, it is enough for me that I am here by the will of him whom I love, who loves me more than all others do, and who knows what is best for me. Sweet is the rest of those who rest in the arms of the divine will.

St. Teresa says the great thing to be acquired by one who practices the habit of prayer is the conformity of his own will with the divine, for in that consists the highest perfection. Therefore, we must be ever repeating to God that prayer of David: "Teach me to do your will" (Ps 143:10). The most perfect act of love which a soul can perform toward God is to ask, "Lord, what will you have me to do?" This ought to be the object of all our works, desires, and prayers, the accomplishment of the divine will. We ought to beg our Blessed Mother, our patron saints and guardian angels to obtain for us the grace to fulfill the will of God. And whenever things which are opposed to our self-love befall us, we may then by one act of resignation gain treasures of merit. Let us accustom ourselves on such occasions to repeat those words which Jesus himself has, by his own example, taught us: "Am I not to drink the cup the Father has given me?" (Jn 18:11) Or, like Job, let us say: "The Lord gave and the Lord has taken away; blessed be the name of the Lord!" (Jb 1:21) A single "Blessed be God" under adverse circumstances is worth more than a thousand thanksgivings when things go smoothly. And here we may say again: Beautiful is the rest of those who rest themselves in the arms of the will of God. For, "No harm befalls the just" (Prv 12:21).

D. Use of Mental Prayer

The *fourth* means for becoming enamored of God is mental prayer. The eternal truths are not discernible by the natural eye, like the things which are visible in this world. They are to be discerned solely by means of meditation and contemplation. Therefore, unless we pause for a certain length of time in order to consider the eternal truths, and more especially our obligation to love God, we shall hardly loose ourselves from the love of creatures to fix our whole love on God. It is in the time of prayer that we understand the worthlessness of earthly things and the value of the good things of heaven. It is then that God inflames with his love those hearts which do not offer resistance to his calls.

There are many, however, who complain that they go to prayer and do not find God. The reason is that they carry with them a heart full of earth. Detach the heart from creatures, says St. Teresa, seek God, and you will find him: "Good is the Lord . . . to the soul that seeks him" (Lam 3:25). Therefore, to find God in prayer, the soul must be stripped of its love for the things of earth; then God will speak to it: "I will lead her into the desert and speak to her heart" (Hos 2:16).

But in order to find God, physical solitude is not enough; that of the heart is necessary too. The Lord one day said to St. Teresa: "I would willingly speak to many souls, but the world makes such a noise in their hearts that my voice cannot make itself heard." When a detached soul is engaged in prayer, truly does God speak to it and make it understand the love which he has borne it. Then the soul, burning with holy love, speaks not. But in that silence how much does it say! The silence of charity says more to God than could be said by the greatest powers of human eloquence: each sigh that it utters is a manifestation of its whole interior. It then seems as if it could not repeat often enough: "My beloved to me, and I to him."

E. Use of Regular Prayer

The *fifth* means of attaining to a high degree of divine love is ordinary prayer. We are poor in all things; but if we pray, we are rich in all things, for God has promised to grant the prayer of him who prays. He says: "Ask, and you will receive" (Mt 7:7). What greater love can one friend show toward another than to say to him, "Ask of me what you will, and I will give it to you"? This is what the Lord says to each one of us. God is Lord of all things. He promises to give us as much as we ask. If, then, we are poor, the fault is our own, because we do not ask him for the graces which we need. It is because of this that mental prayer is morally necessary for all: for when prayer is laid aside while we are involved in this world's cares, we pay too little attention to the soul; but when we pray, we discover the needs of the soul and then ask for the corresponding graces and obtain them.

The whole life of a saint is one of meditation and prayer. All the graces by means of which they have become saints were received by them in answer to their prayers. If, therefore, we would be saved and become saints, we should knock perseveringly at the gates of the divine Mercy to beg and pray for all that we need. We need humility: let us ask for it and we shall be humble. We need patience under tribulation: let us ask for it and we shall be patient. Divine love is what we desire: let us ask for it and we shall obtain it. "Ask, and you will receive" is God's promise which cannot fail. And Jesus Christ, in order to inspire us with greater confidence in our prayers, has promised us that whatever graces we shall ask of the Father in his name, the Father will give us all of them: "Whatever you ask the Father, he will give you in my name" (Jn 16:23). And in another place he says: "Anything you ask me in my name I will do" (Jn 14:14).

Let a soul be as cold as it can be in divine love; if it has faith, I do not know how it is possible for it not to feel urged to love Jesus Christ. Scripture tells us of the love which he has manifested toward us in his Passion, and in the most holy sacrament of the altar. As regards his Passion, we read in Isaiah: "It was our infirmities that he bore, our sufferings that he endured" (53:4), and in the verse which follows: "He was pierced for our offenses, crushed for our sins." Jesus Christ has willed to suffer in his own Person our pains and afflictions to set us free. And why has he done so, if not for his love for us? "Christ loved you. He gave himself for us" (Eph 5:2), St. Paul says. And St. John: "Christ . . . loves us and freed us from our sins by his own blood" (Rv 1:5). While with respect to the sacrament of the Eucharist, it was Jesus himself who said to us all, when he instituted it, "This is my body, which is for you" (1 Cor 11:24). And in another passage: "The man who feeds on my flesh and drinks my blood remains in me, and I in him" (Jn 6:56). How can anyone who has faith read this without feeling himself, as it were, forced to love his Redeemer who, after having sacrificed his blood and life out of love for him, has left him his own body in the sacrament of the altar to be the food of his soul?

Let us conclude with this brief reflection on the Passion of Jesus Christ. He shows himself to us on the Cross, pierced by three nails, agonizing in the pangs of death. Why all this suffering? Is it, perhaps, that we might pity him? No, it is not so much to gain our compassion as to become the object of our love that he has reduced himself to such a state. It should have been enough to secure our love had he shown us that his love for us is from all eternity: "With age-old love I have loved you" (Jer 31:3). But seeing that this was not enough for our lukewarmness, the Lord has given us a practical demonstration of his love: We see him covered with wounds, dying of anguish through his love for us, that by means of his sufferings we might understand the immensity and tenderness of the love which he has for each of us.

conformity

to the will

of god

I
WHAT IT MEANS

If we wish to satisfy the heart of God, we must in everything bring our own will into conformity with his. We must also strive to bring our will into uniformity with his, as regards all that he commands. Conformity means the joining of our own will to the will of God. Uniformity means, further, making the divine will one with ours, so that we desire nothing but what God desires. This is the sum and substance of that perfection to which we ought to aspire; this is what must be the aim of all our works, desires, meditations, and prayers. For this we must ask the assistance of all our patron saints and of our guardian angels, and above all of our Mother Mary, who was the most perfect of all the saints because she most perfectly embraced the divine will.

But the chief point lies in our embracing the will of God in all things which befall us, not only when they are favorable, but when they are contrary to our desires. When things go well, even sinners find no difficulty in being in a state of uniformity to the divine will; but the saints are in uniformity also under circumstances which run counter to self-love. It is in this that the perfection of our love for God is shown.

We must bring ourselves into uniformity to the divine will, not only as regards those adverse circumstances which come to us directly from God — such as sickness, poverty, the death of loved ones and other things of a similar nature — but also as regards those which come to us through men, such as insults, acts of injustice, thefts and persecutions. We must understand, when someone damages our reputation, our honor, or our property, that although the Lord does not will the sin which such a one commits, he nevertheless does will our humiliation, our poverty, and our mortification. It is certain that everything which comes to pass in the world comes to pass through the divine will: "I form the light, and create the darkness, I make well-being and create woe" (Is 45:7). From God come all things that are good and all things that are evil, that is to say, all things which are contrary to our own liking and which we falsely call evil; for they are good when we receive them as coming from his hands: "If evil befalls a city, has not the Lord caused it?" said the prophet Amos (3:6). "Good and evil, life and death, poverty and riches, are from the Lord" (Sir 11:14).

It is true, as I observed above, that whenever anyone treats you unjustly, God does not will the sin which such a person commits, or concur in the malice of his intentions. But he concurs as regards the material action by which such a person wounds, plunders, or injures you, so that what you have to suffer is certainly willed by God and comes to you from his hands. Thus the Lord told David that he was the author of the injuries which Absalom would inflict upon him, even to the taking away of his wives in his very presence, in punishment for his sins: "I will bring evil upon you out of your own house. I will take your wives while you live to see it, and will give them to your neighbor" (2 Sm 12:11). He also told the Israelites that it would be as a punishment for their wickedness when he would command the Assyrians to spoil and bring them to ruin: "Woe to Assyria! My rod in anger, my staff in wrath . . . I order him to seize plunder, carry off loot, and tread them down like the mud of the streets" (Is 10:5-6). St. Augustine explains it thus: "The wickedness of these men is made to be, as it were, an axe of God," to chastise the Israelites. And Jesus himself said to St. Peter that his

Passion and death did not come to him so much from men as from his Father himself: "Am I not to drink the cup the Father has given me?" (Jn 18:11)

When the messenger came to Job to tell him that the Sabeans had taken all his goods away, and had put his sons to death, what was his reply? "The Lord gave and the Lord has taken away" (Jb 1:21). He did not say the Lord has given me sons and property and the Sabeans have taken them away from me; but the Lord has given them to me, and the Lord has taken them away. He perfectly understood that his loss was willed by God; and therefore he added, "Blessed be the name of the Lord!" We must not look upon the troubles which befall us as happening by chance, or only through the fault of others. We must rest assured that everything which happens to us comes to pass through the divine will.

He who acts in this way does not only become a saint, but he enjoys, even in this world, a perpetual peace. The happiest man in the world is he who abandons himself to the will of God and receives all things, whether prosperous or adverse, as from his hands. "We know that God makes all things work together for the good of those who have been called . . . " (Rom 8:28). Those who love God are always content, because all their pleasure lies in the accomplishment of the divine will. Thus, even afflictions are converted into contentment by the thought that in the acceptance of them they are giving pleasure to the Lord whom they love: "No harm befalls the just" (Prv 12:21). And, in truth, what greater contentment can a man ever experience than in seeing the accomplishment of all that he desires? Now whenever anyone desires nothing except what God desires, everything that such a one desires does, consequently, come to pass. Souls that are truly resigned desire whatever happens; if they suffer poverty, they desire to be poor. Whatever happens to them, they desire it all; and therefore they are, in this life, happy. When cold or heat, rain or wind prevails, he who is in a state of union with the divine will says: I wish it to be cold, I wish it to be hot; I wish the wind to blow, the rain to fall, because God wishes it so. If poverty, persecution, sickness, death arrive, I also wish to be poor, persecuted, sick; I wish even to die, because God wishes it.

This is the freedom which the sons of God enjoy, worth more than all the wealth of this world. This is that great peace which the saints experience, which "is beyond all understanding" (Phil 4:7), with which the pleasures of the senses and all other worldly satisfactions cannot compete. For these, being unsubstantial and transitory, may bring temporary pleasure to the senses; but they do not bring contentment to the spirit in which true contentment resides, "The godless man, like the moon, is inconstant" (Sir 27:11). The godless, that is the sinner, changes like the moon which today waxes, tomorrow wanes. Today you will see him laughing, tomorrow weeping; today all gentleness, tomorrow furious as a tiger. And why? Because his contentment depends on the prosperity or the adversity with which he meets, and therefore he varies as the circumstances which befall him vary. But the just man is like the sun, always constant in his serenity under whatever circumstances may come to pass, because his contentment lies in his uniformity with the divine will. Therefore he enjoys a peace which nothing can disturb. The will of God is good, delightful, and perfect, because he wills only that which is best and most perfect.

How great is the folly of those who fight against the divine will! They have to suffer, because no one can ever prevent the accomplishment of the divine decrees. And they even draw down upon themselves greater punishment in the next life and greater unhappiness in this: "Who has withstood him and remained unscathed?" (Jb 9:4) Let the sick man cry as he will about his pains. Let him who is in poverty complain, rave, blaspheme against God as much as he pleases in his distresses — what will he gain by it but the doubling of his affliction? "What are you in search of, foolish man," says St. Augustine, "when seeking good things? Seek that one good in whom are all good things." What can you find, senseless man, away from your God? Find God, unite yourself to his will; and you will always be happy, both in this life and in the next.

In short, what is there that God wills but our good? Whom can we ever find to love us more than he? It is his will, not merely that no one should perish, but that all should save and sanctify themselves: "He wants none to perish but all to come to repentance" (2 Pt 3:9). "It is God's will that you grow in holiness" (1 Thes 4:3). It is in our good that God has placed his own glory. It being the nature of goodness to communicate itself, God has a supreme desire to make the souls of men partakers of his own happiness and glory. And if, in this life, he sends us tribulations, they are all for our own good: "God makes all things work together for the good of those who have been called ... " (Rom 8:28). Even punishments do not come to us from God for our destruction but for our salvation. In order to save us from eternal evils, the Lord encircles us with his own good will: "You surround him with the shield of your good will" (Ps 5:13). He not only desires but is anxious for our salvation: "The Lord thinks of me" (Ps 40:18). And what is there that God will ever refuse us, says St. Paul, after having given us his own Son? (Rom 8:32) This, then, is the confidence with which we ought to abandon ourselves to the divine will.

II
HOW TO PRACTICE IT

But let us now look at the matter from a more practical point of view, and consider the circumstances which call for our uniformity with the will of God.

In the first place, we must have this uniformity as regards those things of nature which come to us from without, as when there is great heat, great cold, rain, drought, pestilence, and the like. We must take care not to say: What intolerable heat! What wretched weather! or other such words. We ought to will everything to be as it is, since God orders it all. St. Francis Borgia, on going one night to a Jesuit residence when the snow was falling, knocked at the door several times. But the Fathers were asleep and he was not let in. They apologized in the morning for having kept him waiting outside. But the saint said that during that time he had been consoled by the thought that it was God who was sending those flakes of snow.

In the second place, we must have this uniformity as regards things which happen to us from within, as in the sufferings that come from hunger, thirst, poverty or disgrace. We should always say, "Lord, I am content; I will only what you will."

In the third place, if we have any natural defect either in mind or body — a bad memory, slowness of comprehension, a crippled limb, or weak health — let us not complain. What were we entitled to? What obligation had God to give us a mind more richly endowed, or a body more perfectly made? Could he not have created us mere brute animals or have left us in our own nothingness? Who ever receives a gift and tries to make bargains about it? We should give him thanks for what, through a pure act of his goodness, he has bestowed upon us; we should be content with the manner in which he has treated us. Who can tell, if God had given us more ability, better health, or more beauty and charm, whether we should not have used them to our destruction? How many there are whose ruin has been brought about by their talents and learning; they have grown proud, looked upon others with contempt. How many others there are whose personal beauty or bodily strength have caused them to fall into sin. And, on the contrary, how many others there are who, as a result of their poverty or illness or ugliness, have sanctified themselves and been saved. We should, therefore, be content with that which God has given us: "One thing only is required" (Lk 10:41). Beauty is not necessary, nor health, nor keenness of intellect; what alone is necessary is our salvation.

In the fourth place, we must be particularly resigned under the pressure of sickness. We must embrace it willingly, whatever kind it is and for as long as God wills.

81

Nevertheless, we should employ the usual remedies, for this is what the Lord wills too. But if they do us no good, let us unite ourselves with the will of God, and this will do us much more good than health. Lord, we should say, I have no wish either to get well or to remain sick; I will only what you will. Certainly our virtue is greater if in times of sickness we do not complain of our sufferings. But when these press heavily upon us, it is not a fault to make them known to our friends, or even to ask God to free us from them. I am speaking now of sufferings that are severe. Even Jesus Christ, on seeing the approach of his Passion, said, "My heart is nearly broken with sorrow" (Mt 26:38), and he prayed to be free from it: "My Father, if it is possible, let this cup pass me by" (Mt 26:39). But Jesus himself has taught us what we ought to do after praying in this manner: We must immediately resign ourselves to the divine will, adding, as he did, "Still, let it be as you would have it, not as I."

How foolish, too, are those who say that they wish for health in order to render greater service to God by serving the community, by going to church, by receiving Holy Communion, by doing penance, by study. But, my friend, I wish you would tell me why it is that you want to do these things? Is it to please God? And why go out of your way in order to do them, if you are sure that what pleases God is not that you pray, receive Communion, do acts of penance or study, but that you suffer with patience the sickness or pains which he has sent you? Unite your own sufferings with those of Jesus Christ. But, you say, I am troubled that I am useless, and a burden to my family. Here, too, you should resign yourself to the will of God, and urge your family to resign themselves also. No, these desires and regrets do not spring from the love of God, but from the love of self, which is forever hunting excuses to depart from the will of God. If we wish to give pleasure to God, let us say, whenever we happen to be confined to our beds, "Your will be done." And let us often repeat it, even for the hundredth or thousandth time. In this way we shall give more pleasure to God than we could give him by all the mortifications and devotions which we could perform. There is no better way of serving God than by cheerfully embracing his will. God is not glorified so much by our works as by our resignation and conformity to his holy will. And that is why St. Francis de Sales used to say that we serve God more by suffering than by working.

I call the time of sickness the touchstone by which souls are tried, because in it is discovered the value of the virtue which anyone possesses. If he does not lose his tranquillity, if he makes no complaints, is not overanxious and obeys his doctors, preserving throughout his peacefullness of mind in perfect resignation to the divine will, it is a sign that he possesses great virtue. But what, then, should we say of the sick person who complains and says that he receives little help from others, that his sufferings are intolerable, that he can find no remedy, that his doctor is ignorant, at times complaining even to God that his hand presses too heavily upon him? St. Bonaventure relates, in his life of St. Francis, that when the saint was suffering pains of an extraordinary severity, one of his religious, who was somewhat too simple, said to him: "Father, pray God to treat you with a little more gentleness; for it seems that he lays his hand too heavily upon you." St. Francis, on hearing this, said in reply: "Listen. If I did not know that these words of yours were the result of mere simplicity, I would never look at you again — daring, as you have, to find fault with the judgments of God." And after saying this, extremely weak though he was, he threw himself on the floor and said: "Lord, I thank you for all the sufferings which you send me. I ask you to send me more of them, if it so please you. It is my delight for you to afflict me, because the fulfillment of your will is the greatest consolation which I can receive in this life."

And in the same way we should receive all other crosses from the hands of God. But so many troubles, you say, are punishments. I ask in reply, are not the punishments which God sends us in this life acts of kindness? If we have offended him, we have to satisfy his justice in some way or other, either in this life or in the next. It should be a consolation to one who has deserved hell to see that God is punishing him in this world. This should give him hope that it may be God's will to deliver him from eternal punishment. Let us, then, say what was said by Eli, the priest: "He is the Lord. He will do what he judges best" (1 Sm 3:18).

In times of spiritual desolation, we should also be resigned. When a soul first gives itself up to the spiritual life, the Lord is accustomed to heap consolations upon it and thus withdraw it from the pleasures of the world. But afterward, when he sees it more settled in spiritual ways, he draws back his hand to test its love, and to see whether it serves and loves him without reward in this world. "While we are living here," as St. Teresa used to say, "our reward does not consist in any increase of our enjoyment of God, but in the performance of his will." And in another passage: "The love of God does not consist in tenderness, but in serving him with firmness and humility." And: "The Lord tries those who love him by means of dryness and temptations." Let the soul thank the Lord when he caresses it with sweetness, but not torment itself with impatience when it is left in a state of desolation.

This is a point which should be well understood, for some foolish persons, seeing themselves in a state of dryness, think that God may have abandoned them, and so they stop praying and lose all that they have gained. There is no better time for exercising our resignation to the will of God than when we suffer spiritual dryness. I am not saying that you will not suffer pain on seeing yourself deprived of the sensible presence of God. It is impossible for a soul not to feel such pain as this. Even our Redeemer cried out from the Cross: "My God, my God, why have you forsaken me?" (Mt 27:46) In its sufferings such a soul should always resign itself perfectly to the will of the Lord. These spiritual desolations and abandonments are what all the saints have suffered. "What hardness of heart," said St. Bernard, "do I not experience! I no longer find any delight in reading, no longer any pleasure in meditation or in prayer." The condition of the saints has been, ordinarily, one of dryness. Consolations the Lord does not bestow, except on rare occasions, and to perhaps the weaker ones, in order to prevent their coming to a standstill in their spiritual journey. The joys which he promises as rewards are being prepared for us in heaven. This world is the place for meriting by suffering; heaven is the place for rewards and enjoyments. Therefore, what the saints have desired and sought for in this world has been not a sensible fervor with rejoicing, but a spiritual fervor with suffering.

We must bear in mind that dryness is not

always a punishment, but is occasionally sent by God for our greater good, in order to keep us humble. When God sends darkness and desolation, he is testing his true friends. This, then, is your answer whenever you feel yourself tempted to stop praying because it seems to be a waste of time: "I am here in order to please God." St. Francis de Sales used to say that if in time of prayer we did no more than drive away distractions and temptations, our prayer would be well made.

What is said with regard to dryness, must also be said of temptations. We should try to avoid temptations; but if God wills or permits that we be tempted against the faith, against purity, or against any other virtue, we should not complain, but resign ourselves in this also to the divine will. To St. Paul, who prayed to be released from his temptations, the Lord answered: "My grace is sufficient for you." And so, if we see that God does not listen to us by releasing us from some temptation, let us also say: Lord, do whatever pleases you; your grace is sufficient for me. Temptations are not the cause of our losing divine grace. Temptations, when we overcome them, keep us more humble, gain for us greater merits, make us have recourse to God more frequently, and thus keep us from offending him and unite us more closely to his holy love.

We must also unite ourselves with the will of God in regard to our death, and as to the time and manner in which he will send it. What is this world but a prison for us to suffer in, and to be in danger every moment of losing God? This is what caused the Psalmist to exclaim: "Lead me forth from prison" (Ps 142:8). It was this fear which made St. Teresa sigh for death; on hearing the clock strike, she felt consolation in the thought that an hour of her life had passed, an hour of her danger of losing God. What is more precious, or to be more desired, than by a good death to secure the impossibility of losing the grace of our God? But you say, "I have as yet done nothing; there is nothing that I have gained for my soul." But if it be the will of God for your life to terminate at this time, what would you do afterward if you were to remain alive contrary to his will? Who knows whether, through a change of will, you might not fall into other sins and lose eternal life?

I say that he who has but little desire for heaven shows that he has but little love for God. One who loves desires the presence of the object loved. But we cannot see God without leaving this world, and that is why all the saints have longed for death, in order to go and see the Lord whom they have loved. And so Augustine said, "O, may I die, that I may see you!" And St. Paul wrote, "I long to be freed from this life and to be with Christ" (Phil 1:23).

Finally, although we ought to value the glory of God, we ought to value his will even more. It is right for us to desire to love him more than the angels do, but it is not right for us to wish for any other degree of love than that which the Lord has granted us. It would be an obvious fault to desire to possess gifts of supernatural prayer, such as ecstasies, visions, and revelations. On the contrary, spiritual writers say that those souls on which God bestows the favor of such graces ought to pray to be deprived of them so that they may love him by the way of pure faith. There are many who have attained perfection without these supernatural graces. The only virtues are those which raise the soul to sanctity, and chief among them stands uniformity with the will of God. If God does not choose to raise us to a high degree of perfection and of glory, let us conform ourselves to his holy will, praying that he would at least save us through his mercy. And if we act in this manner, that reward will not be small which our good Lord will give us, since he loves above all those souls that are resigned.

In short, we ought to regard all things that do or will happen to us as proceeding from God's hands; and everything that we do we should direct to this one end: the fulfillment of his will. Above all, let us serve God in the way in which he wills. I say this so that we may shun the deception practiced by one who loses time amusing himself by saying: "If I were in a desert, if I were to enter a monastery, if I were to go somewhere else, I would sanctify myself; I would do such and such a penance; I would say such and such prayers." He says, "I would do, I would do." But in the meantime, by bearing with a bad will the cross which God sends him, he not only does not sanctify himself, but goes from bad to worse. These desires are temptations of the devil. We must therefore drive them away and embrace the service of God in that one way which he has chosen for us. By doing his will, we shall certainly sanctify ourselves in any state in which God places us. We should, then, always will only that which God wills, so that we may be entirely his.

Let us make ourselves familiar with some of those passages of Scripture which call us to unite ourselves ever more and more with the divine will: "I am yours; save me" (Ps 119:94). And especially at times when any very great calamity befalls us — as in the case of the death of parents, of the loss of property, and other such things, let us say: "Father, it is true. You have graciously willed it so" (Mt 11:26). And, above all, let us love that prayer which Jesus Christ has taught us: "Your will be done on earth as it is in heaven." Our Lord told St. Catherine of Genoa that, whenever she said the "Our Father," she was to pay particular attention to these words, and pray that his holy will might be fulfilled by her. Let us, too, act in this manner, and we shall certainly become saints ourselves.

thoughts

on the

incarnation

God Sent His Own Son

Consider how God allowed 4,000 years to pass after the sin of Adam before he sent his Son on earth to redeem the world. And in the meantime, what fatal darkness reigned on the earth! The true God was not known or adored, except in one small corner of the world. Idolatry reigned everywhere; devils and beasts and stones were adored as gods. But let us admire in this the divine wisdom: He deferred the coming of the Redeemer so that the event might be more welcome to man, and so that the malice of sin as well as the necessity of a remedy and of the grace of the Savior might be better known. If Jesus Christ had come into the world immediately after the Fall of Adam, the greatness of this favor would have been but slightly appreciated. Let us, therefore, thank the goodness of God for having sent us into the world after the great work of redemption was accomplished.

Behold the happy time is come which was called the designated time: "When the designated time had come, God sent his Son . . . to deliver from the law those who were subjected to it" (Gal 4:4). It is called the fullness of time because of the fullness of grace which the Son of God came to communicate to men by the redemption of the world.

Picture the angel who is sent as ambassador into the town of Nazareth to announce to the Virgin Mary the coming of the Word who desires to become incarnate in her womb. The angel salutes her, calls her full of grace and blessed among women. The humble Virgin, chosen to be the Mother of the Son of God, is troubled at these praises because of her great humility. But the angel encourages her, and tells her that she has found grace with God, the grace which brought peace between God and man and the reparation of the ruin caused by sin. He then tells her that she must give her Son the name of Savior — "You shall give him the name Jesus" — and that this, her Son, is the very Son of God who is to redeem the world and thus to reign over the hearts of men.

At last Mary consents to be the Mother of such a Son: "Let it be done to me as you say." And the eternal Word takes flesh and becomes Man: "And the Word became flesh." Let us thank this Son, and let us also thank his Mother, who, in consenting to be Mother of such a Son, consented also to be Mother of our salvation, and Mother also of sorrows, accepting at that time the great sorrows that it would cost her to be the Mother of a Son who was to come into the world to suffer and die for man.

He Took the Form of a Slave

The eternal Word descends on earth to save man; and from where does he descend? "At one end of the heavens it comes forth" (Ps 19:7). He descends from the bosom of his divine Father, where from eternity he was begotten in the brightness of sanctity. And where does he descend? He descends into the womb of a Virgin, a child of Adam, which in comparison with the bosom of God is an object of horror. Therefore, the Church sings, "You did not abhor the Virgin's womb." Yes, because the Word is God, he is immense, omnipotent, most blessed, and supreme Lord, and equal in everything to the Father. But in the womb of Mary he is a creature, small, weak, afflicted, a slave inferior to the Father.

It is related as a great sign of humility in St. Alexis that, although he was the son of a Roman gentleman, he chose to live as a servant in his father's house. But how is the humility of this saint to be compared to the humility of Jesus Christ? Between the son and the servant of the father of St. Alexis there was, it is true, some difference; but between God and the servant of God, there is an infinite difference.

Besides, this Son of God, the servant of his Father, in obedience to him made himself also the servant of his creatures, Mary and Joseph: "And [he] was obedient to them" (Lk 2:51). Moreover, he made himself even a servant of Pilate, who condemned him to death, and he was obedient to him and accepted it; he became a servant to the executioners, who scourged him, crowned him with thorns and crucified him; and he humbly obeyed them all, and yielded himself into their hands. And shall we, after this, refuse to submit ourselves to the service of so loving a Savior, who, to save us, has subjected himself to such painful and degrading slavery?

He Gave Himself Out of Love

Consider that the eternal Word is that God who is so infinitely happy in himself that his happiness cannot be greater than it is, nor could the salvation of all mankind have added anything to it or have diminished it. And yet he has done and suffered so much to save us that if his happiness (as St. Thomas says) had depended on that of man, he could not have done or suffered more: "As if without him he could not be happy." And, indeed, if Jesus Christ could not have been happy without redeeming us, how could he have humbled himself more than he has done, in taking upon himself our infirmities, the miseries of infancy, the troubles of human life, and a death so barbarous and ignominious? None but God was capable of loving to such an excess such sinners as we are, so unworthy of being loved.

A devout author says that if Jesus Christ had permitted us to ask him to give us the greatest proof of his love, who would have ventured to ask of him that he should become a child like us, that he should clothe himself with all our miseries, and make himself, of all men, the most poor, the most despised, and the most ill-treated? Who would have dared to ask that he should be put to death by the hands of executioners, cursed and forsaken by all, even by his own Father, who abandoned his Son that he might not abandon us in our ruin? But that which we should not have had the boldness even to think of, the Son of God has thought of and accomplished. Even from his childhood he has sacrificed himself for us to sufferings, to disgrace, and to death. He has loved us; and out of love has given us himself, in order that we, by offering him as a Victim to the Father in satisfaction for our debts, might through his merits obtain from the divine Goodness all the graces that we desire. Let us, therefore, continually offer to God the merits of Jesus Christ, and through them let us seek and hope for every good.

He Knew He Was to Suffer

The prophet Isaiah designates our Lord Jesus Christ as "a man of suffering" because this Man was created on purpose to suffer, and from his infancy began to endure the greatest sorrows that any man ever suffered. The first man, Adam, enjoyed for some time upon this earth the delights of the earthly paradise; but the second Adam, Jesus Christ, did not pass a moment of his life without sorrows and anguish. Even from his childhood he was afflicted by the foresight of all the sufferings and ignominy that he would have to endure during his life, and especially at his death, when he was to close that life immersed in sorrow and disgrace, as David had predicted: "I have reached the watery depths; the flood overwhelms me" (Ps 69:3).

Indeed, from the womb of Mary, Jesus Christ accepted obediently the sacrifice which his Father had desired of him, even his Passion and death, "obediently accepting even death" (Phil 2:8). He foresaw the scourges, and presented to them his flesh; he foresaw the thorns, and presented to them his head; he foresaw the blows, and presented to them his cheeks; he foresaw the nails, and presented to them his hands and his feet; he foresaw the Cross, and offered his life. Hence it is true that even from his earliest infancy our blessed Redeemer, every moment of his life, suffered a continual martyrdom, and he offered it every moment for us to his eternal Father.

But what afflicted him most was the sight of the sins which men would commit even after this painful redemption. By his divine light he knew well the malice of every sin, and therefore he came into the world to do away with all sins; but when he saw the immense number which would be committed, the sorrow that Jesus felt was greater than all the sorrows that all men ever suffered, or ever will suffer, upon earth.

He Foresaw His Life of Sorrow

Consider the great bitterness which the infant Jesus must have felt in Mary's womb at the first moment when his Father proposed to his consideration all the contempt, sorrow, and agonies which he was to suffer during his life to deliver men from their miseries: "Morning after morning he opens my ear ... And I have not rebelled ... I gave my back to those who beat me" (Is 50:4-6). Picture Jesus speaking by the mouth of the prophet: "Morning after morning he opens my ear," that is, from the first moment of my conception my Father made me feel that it was his will that I should lead a life of sorrows and in the end be sacrificed on the Cross. "And I have not rebelled ... I gave my back to those who beat me." And all this I accepted for your salvation, and from that time onward I gave up my body to the scourges, to the nails, and to the death on the Cross.

Consider that whatever Jesus Christ suffered in his life and in his Passion was all placed before him while he was still in the womb of Mary, and he accepted everything that was proposed to him with delight. But in accepting all this, and in overcoming the natural repugnance of sense, what anguish and oppression the innocent heart of Jesus must have suffered! He well understood all he was to endure: the shame and the sorrows of his birth, being born in a cold grotto that was a stable for beasts; the humble life he was to lead for 30 years in the shop of an artisan; the treatment he would receive, considered to be ignorant, a slave, a seducer, and one guilty of death. All this did our Redeemer accept every moment; but each moment that he accepted it he suffered at once all the pains and humiliations that he would afterward endure. The very knowledge of his divine dignity made him feel even more the injuries he would receive from men: "All the day my disgrace is before me" (Ps 44:16). He had continually before his eyes his shame, especially that confusion which he would one day feel at seeing himself stripped naked, scourged, and suspended by three iron nails, and so to end his life in the midst of the insults and curses of those very men for whom he was to die, "obediently accepting even death, death on a cross!" (Phil 2:8)

And for what? To save us miserable and ungrateful sinners.

He Was Born in a Stable

The Church, in contemplating this great mystery of a God being born in a stable, exclaims, full of admiration, "Oh, great mystery! Oh, wonderful sacrament! for animals to behold the Lord lying in a manger."

In order to contemplate with tenderness and love the birth of Jesus, we must pray to the Lord for a lively faith. If without faith we enter into the grotto of Bethlehem, we shall have nothing but a feeling of compassion at seeing an infant reduced to such a state of poverty that being born in the depth of winter, he is laid in a manger of beasts, without fire, and in the midst of a cold cavern. But if we enter with faith, and consider with what an excess of love it was that God humbled himself to appear like a little child, wrapped in swaddling clothes, placed on straw, crying and shivering with cold, unable to move, depending for subsistence on his mother's milk, how then is it possible for us not to feel gently constrained to give all our affections to this infant God who has reduced himself to this state to make us love him!

St. Luke says that the shepherds, after having visited Jesus in the manger, "returned, glorifying and praising God for all they had heard and seen" (Lk 2:20).

And yet what had they seen? Nothing more than a poor Child trembling with cold on a little straw. But being enlightened by faith, they recognized in this Child the excess of divine love. Inflamed by this love they went on their way glorifying God, for they had had the happiness to behold a God "who had emptied himself" and annihilated himself for the love of men.

He Came as a Child,
That We Might Love Him More

Consider that after so many centuries, after so many prayers, the Messiah, whom the holy patriarchs and prophets were not worthy to see, whom the nations longed for, "the desire of the everlasting hills," our Savior has come; he is already born, and has given himself entirely to us: "A child is born to us, a son is given us" (Is 9:5). The Son of God has made himself little, in order to make us great. He has given himself to us, in order that we may give ourselves to him. He has come to show us his love, in order that we may respond to it by giving him ours.

Let us, therefore, receive him with affection. Let us love him, and present to him all our needs. "A child gives easily," says St. Bernard; children readily give anything that is asked of them. Jesus came into the world as a child in order to show himself ready and willing to give us all good gifts: "The Father has given all things to him." If we wish for light, he has come on purpose to enlighten us. If we wish for strength to resist our enemies, he has come to give us comfort. If we wish for pardon and salvation, he has come to pardon and save us. If, in short, we desire the sovereign gift of divine love, he has come to inflame our hearts with it; and for this very purpose, he has become a Child, and has chosen to show himself to us worthy of our love, in order to take away from us all fear and to gain our affections.

Jesus has chosen to come as a little Child to make us love him, not only with an appreciative but even a tender love. All infants attract the tender affection of those who see them; but who will not love, with all the tenderness of which they are capable, a God whom they behold as a little child, in need of milk to nourish him, trembling with cold, poor, abased, and forsaken, weeping and crying in a manger, and lying on straw? It was this that made the loving St. Francis exclaim: "Let us love the Child of Bethlehem, let us love the Child of Bethlehem. Come, souls, and love a God who has become a Child, poor and so lovable, who has come down from heaven to give himself entirely to you."

The Magi Visit Jesus

The Son of God is born humble and poor in a stable; there the angels of heaven acknowledge him, singing, "Glory to God in the highest." But the inhabitants of the earth, for whose salvation Jesus was born, leave him neglected; only a few shepherds come and acknowledge him to be their Savior. But our loving Redeemer desired from the very beginning to communicate to us the grace of redemption, and therefore he began to make himself known even to the gentiles, who neither knew him nor expected him. For this reason he sent the star to give notice to the holy Magi, enlightening them at the same time with internal light, in order that they might come and acknowledge and adore him as their Redeemer. This was the first grace bestowed upon us: our calling to the true faith. Oh, Savior of the world, what would have become of us if you had not come to enlighten us? We should be like our forefathers who worshiped animals, stones, and wood. I give you thanks today on behalf of all men.

The Magi, without delay, set out on their journey, and by means of the star they arrived at the place where the holy Infant lay: "They found the child with Mary his mother" (Mt 2:11). As they looked on the Child, they felt an interior joy, and their hearts were drawn toward him. The poverty and the cries of the Child were darts of love and fire to their enlightened hearts. Yes, Jesus, the more humbled and poor I behold you, the more you inflame me with your love.

The Child looked at these holy pilgrims with a joyful face, and thus showed that he accepted these first fruits of his redemption. His Mother was also silent, but by her smiling looks she welcomed them and thanked them for the homage done to her Son. They adored him in silence, and acknowledged him for their Savior and their God, offering him gifts of gold, frankincense and myrrh. Jesus, I also adore you and offer you my whole heart. Take it and change it. Make it entirely yours, so that it may love nothing but you. Save me, and let my salvation be to love you always and without reserve. Mary, most holy Virgin, I hope for this grace from you.

His Life in Nazareth

St. Joseph, on his return to Palestine, heard that Archelaus reigned in Judea instead of his father, Herod. Therefore, he was afraid to go and live there. Having been warned in a dream, he went to live in Nazareth, a city of Galilee, and there in a poor little cottage he fixed his dwelling. In this house, the Incarnate Word lived during the remainder of his infancy and youth. And how did he live? Poor and despised by men, performing the offices of a common working boy, and obeying Joseph and Mary: "And [he] was obedient to them" (Lk 2:51).

How inspiring it is to think that in this poor house the Son of God lived as a servant, fetching water, opening and shutting the shop, sweeping the floor. It is a thought that ought to make us all burn with holy love for our Redeemer, who has reduced himself to such humiliations in order to gain our love. Let us adore all these servile actions of Jesus, which were all divine. Let us adore, above all, the hidden and neglected life that Jesus Christ led in the house of Nazareth. Proud men, how can you desire to make yourselves seen and honored, when you see your God spend years of his life in poverty, hidden and unknown, to teach us the love of retirement and of a humble and hidden life!

Jesus Is Lost in the Temple

St. Luke relates in his Gospel that Mary and Joseph went every year to Jerusalem on the feast of the Passover, and took the infant Jesus with them. It was the custom, says the Venerable Bede, for the Jews making this pilgrimage to travel with the men separated from the women, and the children went with either their fathers or their mothers.

Our Redeemer, who was then twelve years old, remained during this solemnity for three days in Jerusalem. Mary thought he was with Joseph, and Joseph that he was with Mary. The holy Child spent all these three days in honoring his eternal Father by fasts, vigils and prayers, and by assisting at the sacrifices. If he took a little food, says St. Bernard, he must have obtained it by begging, and if he took any rest, he could have had no other bed than the bare ground.

When Mary and Joseph arrived in the

evening at their home, they did not find Jesus, and so they began to look for him among their relations and friends. At last, returning to Jerusalem, they found him in the Temple disputing with the rabbis who, full of astonishment, admired the questions and answers of this wonderful Child. On seeing him, Mary said, "Son, why have you done this to us? You see that your father and I have been searching for you in sorrow." There is no other sorrow like that which is felt by souls who love Jesus when they fear that Jesus has withdrawn himself from them through some fault of theirs. This was the sorrow of Mary and Joseph which afflicted them so much during these days; they perhaps feared that they had rendered themselves unworthy of the care of such a treasure.

That is why Mary said to him, in order to express this sorrow, "Son, why have you done this to us? You see that your father and I have been searching for you in sorrow." Jesus answered, "Did you not know that I had to be in my Father's house?" Let us learn from this mystery two lessons: the first, that we must leave all our friends and relations when the glory of God is in question; the second, that God easily makes himself found by those who seek him, "Good is the Lord ... to the soul that seeks him" (Lam 3:25).

Jesus Begins to Teach

After 30 years of hidden life, the time

came for our Savior to appear in public to preach the heavenly doctrines which he had come from heaven to teach us. Therefore, it was necessary that he should make himself known as the true Son of God. But how many were there who acknowledged and honored him as he deserved? Besides the few disciples who followed him, the majority, instead of honoring him, despised him as a vile man and an imposter.

This confirmed in the fullest manner the prophecy of Simeon: "This child is destined to be . . . a sign that will be opposed" (Lk 2:34). Jesus Christ was contradicted and despised by all. He was despised in his doctrine, for when he declared that he was the only begotten Son of God, he was called a blasphemer, and as such was condemned to death — as Caiphas said, "He has blasphemed . . . He deserves death" (Mt 26:65, 66). He was despised in his wisdom, for he was esteemed a fool without sense — "He is possessed by a devil — out of his mind! Why pay any attention to him?" (Jn 10:20) His morals were reproached as being scandalous — they called him a glutton, a drunkard, and the friend of wicked people — "Here is a glutton and a drunkard, a friend of tax collectors and sinners" (Lk 7:34). He was accused of being a sorcerer and of having dealings with devils — "He casts out demons through the prince of demons" (Mt 9:34). He was called a heretic and one possessed by the devil — "Are we not right, after all, in saying you are a

Samaritan, and possessed besides?" (Jn 8:48) In short, Jesus Christ was considered by all the people so wicked a Man that there was no need of a tribunal to condemn him to be crucified — "If he were not a criminal, we would certainly not have handed him over to you" (Jn 18:30).

Jesus Suffers and Dies

At last the Savior came to his Passion and death. What contempt and ill-treatment he received! He was betrayed and sold by one of his own disciples for 30 pieces of silver, less than would be given for an animal. By another disciple he was denied. He was dragged through the streets of Jerusalem bound like a thief, abandoned by all, even by his few remaining disciples. He was treated shamefully as a slave when he was scourged. He was struck on the face in public. He was treated as a fool when Herod had a white garment put on him, that he might be thought a foolish person without any sense: "He despised him as ignorant," says St. Bonaventure, "because he did not answer a word; as foolish, because he did not defend himself." He was treated as a mock king, when they put into his hand a reed instead of a scepter, a tattered red garment upon his shoulders instead of the purple, and a chaplet of thorns on his head for a crown. After thus deriding him, they saluted him: "All hail, king of the Jews!" (Mt 27:29) And then they covered him with spittle and blows.

"They also spat at him" (Mt 27:30); "slapping his face" (Jn 19:3).

Finally, Jesus Christ willed to die; but by what death? By the most shameful death, which was the death of the cross: "He humbled himself, obediently accepting even death, death on a cross!" (Phil 2:8) Anyone who suffered the death of the cross at that time was considered the vilest and most wicked of criminals: "Accursed is anyone who is hanged on a tree" (Gal 3:13). The names of those who were crucified were always held as cursed and infamous, so that the apostle wrote that Christ is made "a curse for us" (Gal 3:13). St. Athanasius, commenting on this passage, says: "He is called a curse, because he bore the curse for us." Jesus took upon himself this curse that he might save us from an eternal curse. But where, Lord, exclaims St. Thomas of Villanova, where is your beauty, where is your majesty in the midst of so much disgrace? And he answers: "Ask not, God has gone out of himself." The saint's meaning was this: We should not seek for glory and majesty in Jesus Christ, since he had come to give us an example of humility and make manifest his love for men. This love had made him, as it were, go out of himself.

In the fables of the pagans, it is related that the god, Hercules, because of his love for King Augea, undertook to tame his horses, and that the god, Apollo, out of love for Admetus, kept his flocks for him.

These are inventions of the imagination, but it is of faith that Jesus Christ, the true Son of God, for the love of men humbled himself to be born in a stable, to lead a contemptible life, and in the end to die by the hands of executioners on an infamous gibbet.

"Oh, power of love!" exclaims St. Bernard. "You, the most high, became the lowest of all!" Oh, the strength of divine love! The greatest of all has made himself the lowest of all! And why? St. Bernard says that it was because of love, regardless of its dignity. "Love triumphs over God." Love does not consider dignity when there is question of gaining for itself the person it loves. God, who can never be conquered by anyone, has been conquered by love; for it was that love which compelled him to make himself Man and to sacrifice himself for the love of man. "He emptied himself," Bernard concludes, "in order that you may know that it was through love that the highest made himself equal to you."

The divine Word, who is majesty itself, humbled himself so far as to annihilate himself, so that men might know how much he loved them. Yes, says St. Gregory Nazianzen, because in no other way could he better show forth the divine love than by abasing himself, and taking upon himself the greatest misery and shame that men ever suffer on this earth. Man had the boldness to offend the majesty of God; in order to expiate his guilt the intervention of the most excessive humiliation was necessary. St. Bernard says, "The lower he showed himself to be in human nature, the greater did he declare himself in goodness."

He Died That We Might Live

Your physician will come, says the prophet, to cure the infirm; and he will come swiftly like the bird that flies, and like the sun which, on rising from the horizon, instantly sends its light to the other pole. But behold him, he is already come. Let us console ourselves, and give thanks to him.

St. Augustine says, "He descends to the bed of the sick," that is to say, he even takes upon himself our flesh, for our bodies are the beds of our infirm souls. Other physicians, if they love their patients, do indeed use all their efforts to cure them; but what physician, in order to cure the sick man, ever took upon himself his disease? Jesus Christ has been that Physician, who charged himself with our infirmities in order to cure them. And he would not content himself with sending another in his place, but chose to come himself to fulfill this charitable office in order to gain for himself all our love: "It was our infirmities that he bore, our sufferings that he endured" (Is 53:4). He chose to heal our wounds with his own blood, and by his death to deliver us from eternal death which we had deserved. In short, he chose to swallow the bitter draught of a life of continual sufferings and a painful death to obtain life for us and deliver us from our many evils: "Am I not to drink the cup the Father has given me?" he said to St. Peter (Jn 18:11).

It was necessary, then, that Jesus Christ should suffer such degradation to heal our pride; that he should embrace such a life of poverty to cure our covetousness; that he should be overwhelmed in a sea of troubles, and even die of pure sorrow, to cure our eagerness for sensual pleasures.

His Sufferings Merited Our Salvation

Consider that since the Father has given us his own Son to be our Mediator and Advocate with him, and the Victim in satisfaction for our sins, we cannot despair of obtaining from God whatever favor we ask of him if we avail ourselves of the help of such a Redeemer. "Has he not also, with him, given us all things?" adds the apostle.

What can God deny us when he has not denied us his Son? None of our prayers deserves to be heard or granted by the Lord, for we deserve punishment, not graces, for our sins. But Jesus Christ, who intercedes for us, and offers for us all the sufferings of his life, his blood, and his death, does indeed deserve to be heard. The Father cannot refuse anything to so dear a Son, who offers him a price of infinite value. He is innocent; all that he pays to divine justice is to satisfy our debts; the satisfaction he offers is infinitely greater than all the sins of men. It would not be just that a sinner should perish who repents of his sins and offers to God the merits of Jesus Christ, who has already atoned for him.

Let us therefore thank God, and hope for all things from the merits of Jesus Christ.

His Death Paid the Price of Our Redemption

The divine Word, from the first instant that he was made Man and an Infant in Mary's womb, offered himself to suffer and die as the ransom of the world: "He surrendered himself to death" (Is 53:12). He knew that all the sacrifices of goats and bulls offered to God in times past had not been able to satisfy for the sins of men, that it required a divine Person to pay the price of their redemption.

"Wherefore, on coming into the world, Jesus said, 'Sacrifice and offering you did not desire, but a body you have prepared for me . . . Then I said . . . I have come'" (Heb 10:5, 7). "My Father," said Jesus, "all the victims already offered to you have not sufficed, nor could they suffice, to satisfy your justice; you have given me this body so that by shedding my blood I might appease you and save men. Behold, I come; I am ready. I accept everything, and I submit myself in everything to your will." Humanly speaking, he felt repugnance, for human nature is opposed to a life and death so full of sufferings and shame. But divinely speaking, since his will was entirely subordinate to the will of his Father, he conquered and accepted everything; and Jesus began from that moment to suffer all the anguish and sorrows that he would have to suffer during all the years of his life.

Thus did our Redeemer act from the very first moment of his entrance into the world. But how have we conducted ourselves toward Jesus since we began as adults to know, by the light of faith, the sacred mysteries of redemption? What thoughts, what designs, what goods have we loved! Pleasures, amusements, vengeance, sensuality — these are the goods that have captured the affections of our hearts. But if we have faith, we must at last change our life and our affections. Let us love a God who has suffered so much for us. Let us recall the sufferings which the heart of Jesus endured for us even from his infancy, for then we shall not be able to love anything else but that heart which has loved us so much.

He Died to Save All Men

St. Paul writes (Ti 2:11) that the grace of God has appeared, offering salvation to all men. The grace which is said here to have appeared is the tender love of Jesus Christ toward men, a love that we have not merited, which, therefore, is called "grace." This love was always the same in God, but it was not always apparent. It was at first

promised in many prophecies, and fore-
shadowed in many ways. But at the birth
of the Redeemer, this divine love did
appear and manifest itself by the eternal
Word showing himself to man as an Infant,
lying on straw, crying, and shivering with
cold. In this way he began to make satisfaction for the penalties we deserved, and so
make known to us the affection which he
has for us by giving up his life for us: "The
way we came to understand love was that
he laid down his life for us" (1 Jn 3:16).

Thus the love of our God appeared to
all. But why is it, then, that all men have
not known it, and that even to this day so
many are ignorant of it? This is the reason:
"The light came into the world, but men
loved darkness rather than light" (Jn 3:19).
They have not known him, and they do not
know him, because they do not wish to
know him, loving the darkness of sin rather
than the light of grace. But let us try not to
be one of these people. If in the past we
have shut our eyes to the light, thinking
little of the love of Jesus Christ, let us now
try to have ever before our eyes the sufferings and death of our Redeemer, in order
to love him who has loved us so much: "As
we await our blessed hope, the appearing of
the glory of the great God and of our
Savior Christ Jesus." We may then justly
expect that paradise which Jesus Christ has
acquired for us by his blood.

At his first coming Jesus appeared as an
Infant, poor and humble, and showed him-

self on earth born in a stable, covered with miserable rags, and lying on straw. But at his second coming he will appear on a throne of majesty: "As . . . 'the Son of Man coming on the clouds of heaven' with power and great glory" (Mt 24:30). Blessed then will they be who have loved him, and unhappy those who have not loved him.

Jesus Wants Our Love

The Jews celebrated a day they called *dies ignis,* the day of fire with which Nehemiah consumed the sacrifice upon his return with his countrymen from the captivity of Babylon. In the same way, Christmas can be called the day of fire, on which a God came as a little Child to light the fire of love in the hearts of men. "I have come to light a fire on the earth" (Lk 12:49). So spoke Jesus Christ, and so it was. Before the coming of the Messiah, who loved God upon earth? He was hardly known in Judea, a corner of the world, and even there, how very few loved him when he came. As for the rest of the world, some worshiped the sun; some, animals; and others, stones. But after the coming of Jesus Christ, the name of God became known everywhere, and was loved by many.

It is a custom with many Christians to anticipate the arrival of Christmas a considerable time beforehand by setting up in their homes a crib to represent the birth of Jesus Christ; but there are few who think of preparing their hearts so that the infant Jesus may be born in them and there find rest. Among these few we would like to be numbered, that we too may be made worthy to burn with that flame which gives contentment on earth and bliss in heaven. Let us now consider how the eternal Word had no other purpose in becoming Man than to inflame us with his divine love. Let us ask light of Jesus Christ and of his holy Mother.

Anyone who loves has no other purpose in loving but to be loved in return. St. Bernard remarks that God, having so dearly loved us, seeks nothing else from us but our love. Therefore, he goes on with this admonition to each one of us: "He has made known his love, so that he may experience yours." You have seen the love which God has borne you in becoming Man, in suffering and dying for you. How long shall it be before God knows by experience and by deeds the love you bear him? Every man, at the sight of a God clothed in flesh choosing to lead a life of such hardship and to suffer such a death, ought to be enkindled with love toward a God so loving. "Oh, that you would rend the heavens and come down, with the mountains quaking before you . . . as when fire makes the water boil!" (Is 63:19; 64:1) Oh, that you, my God, would leave the heavens, the prophet cried out before the arrival of the divine Word on earth, and descend here to become man among us!

You would enkindle such a furnace in the human heart that even the most frozen souls must catch the flame of your blessed love. And, in fact, after the Incarnation of the Son of God, how brilliantly has the fire of divine love shone to many loving souls! It may even be said that God was more loved in one century after the coming of Jesus Christ than in the entire 40 preceding centuries. How many men and women have left wealth and honors to seek the desert or the cloister — that there, in poverty and obscure seclusion, they might give themselves up to the love of their Savior! How many martyrs have jubilantly given themselves to torments and to death! How many young virgins have refused the hands of the great ones of this world in order to go and die for Jesus Christ, and so repay in some measure the affection of a God who became Man and died for love of them!

St. Augustine says that God, in order to captivate the love of men, has cast darts of love into their hearts: "God knows how to take aim at love; he draws the arrow that he may make a lover." What are these arrows? They are all the creatures that we see around us; for God has created them all for man, so that man might love him. Augustine also says, "Heaven and earth and all things tell me to love you." It seemed to the saint that the sun, the moon, the stars, the mountains, the plains, the seas, and the rivers spoke to him and said: Augustine, love God, because God has created us for you, so that you might love him. St. Teresa said that all the fair things which we see — the lakes, the rivers, the flowers, the fruits, the birds — all upbraid us with our ingratitude to God, for all are tokens of the love God bears us.

St. Peter Chrysologus says that our Redeemer took many and various forms to attract the love of man. God, who is unchangeable, appeared as a child in a stable, as a boy in a workshop, as a criminal on a scaffold, and now as bread upon the altar. In these varying guises Jesus chose to exhibit himself to us; but whatever character he assumed, it was always the character of a lover. Tell me, my Lord, is there anything else left for you to devise in order to make yourself loved? "Make known his deeds," cried out Isaiah (12:4). Go, redeemed souls, said the prophet, go and publish everywhere the loving devices of this loving God which he has thought out and executed to make himself loved by man. For after lavishing so many of his gifts upon them, he was pleased to bestow himself, and to bestow himself in so many ways.

"If you desire a cure for your wound," says St. Ambrose, "he is a physician." If you are sick and want to be healed, look at Jesus, who heals you by his blood. "If you are parched with fever, he is a fountain." If the impure flame of worldly affections troubles you, he is a fountain to refresh you with his consolation. "If you fear death, he is life; if you long for heaven, he is the way; in short, if you do not wish to die, he is the life; if you wish heaven, he is the way."

Conformity to His Will
Proves Our Love

If we do not have the strength to desire and seek for sufferings, let us at least try to accept with patience those crosses which God sends us for our good. "Where there is patience, there is God," says Tertullian. Where is God? Give me a soul that suffers with resignation; there is God: "The Lord is close to the brokenhearted" (Ps 34:19). The Lord takes delight in being near those who are afflicted. But what kind of afflicted people? It must be those who suffer in peace and are resigned to the divine will. To such as these God gives true peace which consists, as St. Leo says, in uniting our will to the will of God. St. Bonaventure tells us that the divine will is like honey which makes even bitter things sweet and pleasant. For he who obtains all he wishes has nothing left to desire: "Blessed is he who has everything he desires," says St. Augustine. Therefore, he who wills nothing but what God wills is always happy, for as everything happens by the will of God, the soul has always that which it wills.

And when God sends us crosses, let us not only be resigned, but let us also thank him, since it is a sign that he means to pardon our sins and save us from hell. He who has offended God must be punished; and, therefore, we ought always to beg of him to chastise us in this world, and not in the next. That sinner is to be pitied who does not receive his chastisement in this life. When God does not punish a sinner in this life, it is a sign that he waits to punish him in eternity, where the punishment will have no end.

thoughts

on the

holy spirit

INTRODUCTION

The risen Christ appeared to the apostles while they were awaiting the coming of the Holy Spirit. His visits were distinguished by many remarkable wonders and gifts, principally by the gift of the same Holy Spirit. This gift is a result of our redemption by Christ. Jesus himself made this known to us when he said to his disciples that if he did not die, he could not send us the Holy Spirit: "If I fail to go, the Paraclete will never come to you, whereas if I go, I will send him to you" (Jn 16:7).

We know by faith that the Holy Spirit is the love that the Father and the eternal Word have for each other. Therefore, the gift of love, which the Lord infuses into our souls, and which is the greatest of all gifts, is particularly attributed to the Holy Spirit. As St. Paul says, "The love of God has been poured out in our hearts through the Holy Spirit who has been given to us" (Rom 5:5). Here we will consider the great value of divine love in order that we may desire to obtain it, and endeavor by prayer to be made partakers of it, since God has promised it to him who asks for it with humility. "The heavenly Father [will] give the Holy Spirit to those who ask him" (Lk 11:13).

Love is a Fire that Inflames the Heart

God had ordered, in the Old Law, that there should be a fire kept continually burning on his altar: "The fire on the altar is to be kept burning" (Lv 6:5). St. Gregory says that the altars of God are our hearts, where he desires that the fire of his divine love should always be burning. Therefore, the eternal Father, not satisfied with having given us his Son, Jesus Christ, to save us by his death, also gave us the Holy Spirit, that he might dwell in our souls and keep them constantly on fire with love. Jesus himself declared that he had come into the world to inflame our hearts with this holy fire, and that he desired nothing more than to see it kindled: "I have come to light a fire on the earth. How I wish the blaze were ignited!" (Lk 12:49) Forgetting the injuries and ingratitude he received from men on this earth, when he had ascended into heaven he sent down upon us the Holy Spirit.

Most loving Redeemer, you love us as well in your sufferings and shame as in your kingdom of glory! This is why the Holy Spirit chose to appear in the supper room under the form of tongues of fire. The Church, therefore, teaches us to pray: "May the Holy Spirit inflame us with that fire which our Lord Jesus Christ came to bring on the earth, and which he wished to be ignited." This was the holy fire which inflamed the saints to do such great things for God: to love their enemies, to desire contempt, to deprive themselves of all earthly goods, and to joyfully accept even torments and death. Love cannot remain idle and never says, "This is enough." The soul that loves God desires to do everything in order to please him and to attract his affections. This holy fire is ignited by mental prayer. Therefore, if we desire to burn with love for God, let us love prayer; that is the furnace in which this divine love is enkindled.

Love Is a Light that Enlightens the Soul

One of the greatest evils which the sin of Adam has produced in us is that darkening of our reason which is why the passions can cloud our mind. How miserable is any soul which allows itself to be ruled by passion! Passion is, as it were, a mist, a veil which prevents our seeing the truth. How can he avoid evil who does not know what is evil?

Besides, this darkness increases in proportion to our sins. But the Holy Spirit, who is called "most blessed Light," not only inflames our hearts to love him, he also dispels our darkness, and shows us the vanity of earthly things, the value of eternal goods, the importance of salvation, the worth of grace, the goodness of God, the infinite love which he deserves and the immense love which he bears us.

"The natural man does not accept what is taught by the Spirit of God" (1 Cor 2:14). A man who is absorbed in the pleasures of the world knows little of these truths, and therefore he loves what he ought to hate and hates what he ought to love. St. Teresa said that God is not loved because he is not known. Therefore, the saints were always seeking light from God: "Send forth your light; illuminate my darkness; open my eyes." Yes, because without light we cannot avoid pitfalls nor find God.

Love Is a Fountain that Satisfies

Love is also called "a living fountain, fire, and charity." Christ said to the Samaritan woman: "Whoever drinks the water I give him will never be thirsty" (Jn 4:14). Love is the water which satisfies our thirst; he who loves God with his whole heart does not seek or desire anything else, because in God he finds every good. Therefore, satisfied with God, he often joyfully exclaims, "My God and my all!" My God, you are my whole good. But the Almighty complains that many souls go about seeking fleeting pleasures from creatures and leave him who is the infinite good and source of all joy: "They have forsaken me, the source of living waters; they have dug themselves cisterns, broken cisterns, that hold no water" (Jer 2:13). Therefore, God, who loves us and desires to see us happy, cries out and makes known to all: "If anyone thirsts, let him come to me; let him drink" (Jn 7:37). He who wants to be happy, let him come to me. I will give him the Holy Spirit, who will make him happy both in this life and the next.

The water he speaks of is the Holy Spirit, the substantial love which Jesus Christ promised to send us from heaven after his Ascension: "Here he was referring to the Spirit, whom those that come to believe in him were to receive. There was, of course, no Spirit as yet, since Jesus had not yet been glorified" (Jn 7:39). The key which opens the channels of this blessed water is holy prayer, which obtains every good for us to fulfill the promise, "Ask, and you shall receive." We are blind, poor, and weak; but prayer obtains for us light, strength, and abundance of grace. He who prays receives all he wants. God wants to give us his graces; but he also wants us to pray for them.

Love Is a Dew which Enriches

Holy Church teaches us to pray: "May the infusion of the Holy Spirit cleanse our hearts, and enrich them by the interior sprinkling of his dew." Love enriches the good desires, the holy purposes, and the good works of our souls: these are the flowers and fruits which the grace of the Holy Spirit produces. Love is called dew because it cools the heart of bad passions and of temptations. Therefore the Holy Spirit is called refreshment and pleasing coolness in the heat.

This dew falls on our hearts in time of prayer. A quarter of an hour's prayer is sufficient to appease every passion of hatred or of immoderate love, however strong it may be: "He brings me into the banquet hall and his emblem over me is love" (Song 2:4). Meditation is where love is set in order, so that we love our neighbor as ourselves, and God above everything. He who loves God loves prayer. He who does not love prayer will find it morally impossible to overcome his passions.

Love Is a Pause that Refreshes

Love is also called "in labor rest, in mourning comfort." Love is a pause that refreshes, because the principal work of love is to unite the will of the lover with that of the beloved. To a soul that loves God, in every affront it receives, in every sorrow it endures, in every loss which happens to it, the knowledge that it is the will of its beloved for it to suffer these trials is enough to comfort it. It finds peace and contentment in all tribulations merely by saying: This is the will of my God; this is that peace which surpasses all the pleasures of sense, "God's own peace, which is beyond all understanding" (Phil 4:7).

In this life everyone must carry his cross. But as St. Teresa says, the cross is heavy for him who drags it, not for him who embraces it. Our Lord knows how to strike and how to heal: "He wounds, but he binds up," as Job said (5:18). The Holy Spirit renders even disgraces and torments sweet and pleasant: "Father, it is true. You have graciously willed it so" (Mt 11:26). Thus we ought to say in all adversities, "So be it, Lord, because it is your will." And when the fear of any temporal evil that may befall us alarms us, let us always say: "Do what you wish, my God; whatever you do, I accept it." And it is a good practice to thus offer oneself constantly during the day to God, as St. Teresa did.

Love Gives Us Strength

"Stern as death is love" (Song 8:6). As there is no created strength which can resist death, so there is no difficulty for a loving soul which love cannot overcome. When there is a question of pleasing its beloved, love conquers all. "Nothing is so hard that the fire of love cannot conquer it." This is the most certain way to know if a soul really loves God: if it is as faithful in love when things are going badly as when they are prospering.

St. Francis de Sales said that, "God is

quite as kind when he chastises as when he consoles us, because he does all for love." Indeed, it is when he strikes us most in this life that he loves us most. St. John Chrysostom considered St. Paul more fortunate in chains than caught up into the third heaven. The holy martyrs in the midst of their torments rejoiced and thanked the Lord for the greatest favor that could fall to their lot, that of suffering for his love. And other saints, where there were no tyrants to afflict them, became their own executioners by the penances which they inflicted upon themselves in order to please God. St. Augustine says, "For that which men love, either no labor is felt, or the labor itself is loved."

Love Causes God to Dwell in Our Souls

The Holy Spirit is called "Sweet Guest of the soul." This was the great promise made by Jesus Christ to those who love him when he said: "If you love me, and obey the commands I give you, I will ask the Father and he will give you another Paraclete — to be with you always: The Spirit of truth . . . remains with you and will be within you" (Jn 14:16-17). For the Holy Spirit never leaves a soul if he is not driven away from it.

God, then, dwells in a soul that loves him. But he declares that he is not satisfied unless we love him with our whole heart. St. Augustine tells us that the Roman Senate would not admit Jesus Christ into the number of their gods, because they said that he was a proud God, who would have none other beloved but himself. And so it is. He will have no rivals in the heart that loves him; and when he sees that he is not the only object loved, he is jealous, so to speak. St. James writes of those creatures who divide up the heart which he desires to have all to himself: "Do you suppose it is to no purpose that Scripture says, 'The Spirit he has implanted in us tends toward jealousy'?" (Jas 4:5) In short, as St. Jerome says, Jesus is jealous. Therefore, the heavenly Spouse praises that soul which, like the turtledove, lives in solitude and hidden from the world (Song 2:14). Because he does not want the world to take a part of that love which he wants all to himself, he also praises his spouse by calling her "an enclosed garden" (Song 4:12), a garden closed against all earthly love. Do we doubt that Jesus deserves our whole love? "He gave himself entirely to you," says St. John Chrysostom; "he left nothing for himself." He has given you his blood and his life; there remains nothing more for him to give you.

Love Unites Us with God

As the Holy Spirit, who is uncreated love, is the unbreakable bond which binds the Father to the eternal Word, he also unites the soul with God. "Charity is a virtue," says St. Augustine, "uniting us with God." St. Laurence Justinian exclaims: Love, your bond has such strength that it is able to bind even God and unite him to our souls. The bonds of the world are bonds of death; but the bonds of God are bonds of life and salvation because they unite us with him who is our true and only life.

Before the coming of Jesus Christ, men fled from God and refused to unite themselves to their Creator. But a loving God has drawn them to himself by the bonds of love, as he promised through the prophet Hosea: "I drew them with human cords, with bands of love" (11:4). These bands are the benefits, the lights, the calls to his love, the promises of paradise which he makes to us, the gift which he has bestowed upon us — Jesus Christ in the sacrifice of the Cross and in the sacrament of the altar — and, finally, the gift of his Holy Spirit. Therefore the prophet exclaims, "Loose the bonds from your neck, O captive daughter Zion" (Is 52:2).

Oh my soul, you who are created for heaven, loose yourself from the bonds of earth, and unite yourself to God by the bonds of holy love: "Put on love, which binds the rest together and makes them perfect" (Col 3:14). Love is a bond which unites with itself all other virtues and makes the soul perfect. "Love, and do what you wish," said St. Augustine. Love God, and do what you wish, because he who loves God tries to avoid displeasing his beloved and to do only that which the beloved wishes.

Love Is a Treasure Containing Every Good

Love is that treasure of which the Gospel speaks. We must leave all in order to obtain it, because love makes us sharers in the friendship of God. Oh, man, says St. Augustine, why, then, do you go about seeking good things? Seek only that one Good in which all other good things are contained. But we cannot find God, who is this one Good, if we do not give up the things of the earth. St. Teresa writes, "Detach your heart from creatures, and you will find God." He who finds God finds all that he can desire: "Take delight in the Lord, and he will grant you your heart's requests" (Ps 37:4). The human heart is constantly seeking good things that will make it happy; but if it seeks them from creatures, it will never be satisfied, no matter how many it acquires. If it seeks God alone, God will satisfy all its desires. Who are the happiest people in this world, if not the saints? And why? Because they desire and seek only God.

A tyrant offered money and jewels to St. Clement in order to persuade him to renounce Jesus Christ. The saint exclaimed, "Is God to be put into competition with a little dirt? Blessed is he who knows this treasure of divine love and strives to obtain it. He who obtains it will get rid of everything else that he may have nothing else but God."

Love is a thief which robs us of all earthly affections, so that we can say, "And what else do I desire but you alone, my Lord?"

CONCLUSION

The more we love God, the more holy we become. St. Francis Borgia says prayer introduces divine love into the human heart and mortification withdraws the heart from the world and makes it capable of receiving this holy fire. The more there is of the world in the heart, the less room there is for holy love. The saints have always sought to mortify themselves as much as possible. The saints are few, but we must live with the few if we wish to be saved with the few.

In order to become saints, it is necessary to have the desire to be saints; we must have the desire and the resolution. Some are always desiring, but they never begin to put their hands to the work. "Of these irresolute souls," says St. Teresa, "the devil has no fear." On the other hand, the saint said, "God is a friend of generous souls." The devil tries to make it seem like pride to think of doing great things for God. It would indeed be pride in us to think of doing great things for God if we thought of doing them all by ourselves, trusting in our own strength. But it is not pride to resolve to become saints trusting in God and saying, "I can do all things in him who gives me strength." We must, therefore, have courage, make strong resolutions, and begin. Prayer can do everything. What we cannot do by our own strength, we can do easily with the help of God, who has promised to give us whatever we ask of him: "You may ask what you will — it will be done for you" (Jn 15:7).

the

GLORIES

of

mary

I

HAIL HOLY QUEEN

(In this first part, St. Alphonsus examines the words and phrases of the Hail Holy Queen. *Having established the fact that all prayer leads to love of God and that love of God prompts us to pray, he further indicates that to invoke Mary is one of the best forms of prayer. His purpose here is to establish and confirm our confidence in the Mother of God.)*

Hail, holy Queen, Mother of mercy, hail, our life, our sweetness and our hope. To thee do we cry, poor banished children of Eve: to thee do we sigh, mourning and weeping in this vale of tears. Ah then, our Advocate, turn thine eyes of mercy toward us, and after this our exile, show unto us the blessed fruit of thy womb, Jesus, O merciful, O loving, O sweet Virgin Mary!

Mary Is a Queen of Mercy

The Church honors the Virgin Mary with the glorious title of queen because she has been elevated to the dignity of Mother of the King of kings. If the Son is King, says St. Athanasius, his Mother must necessarily be considered queen. From the moment that Mary consented to become the Mother of the eternal Word, she merited the title of queen of the world and of all creatures. If the flesh of Mary, says St. Arnold, was the flesh of Jesus, how can the Mother be separated from the Son in his kingdom? It thus follows that the regal glory must not only be considered as common to the Mother and the Son, but must even be the same.

Mary, then, is queen, but let all learn for their consolation that she is a mild and merciful queen, desiring the good of all sinners. Therefore, the Church salutes her in prayer and names her the Queen of Mercy. The very name of queen signifies, as Albert the Great remarks, compassion and provision for the poor, differing in this from the title of empress, which signifies severity and rigor. The greatness of kings and queens consists in comforting the wretched so that, whereas tyrants have only their own advantage in view, kings should be concerned with the good of their subjects. Therefore, at the consecration of kings, their heads are anointed with oil, which is the symbol of mercy, to denote that in ruling they should always show kindness and good will toward their subjects.

Kings, then, should principally occupy themselves with works of mercy, but they should not neglect the exercise of justice toward the guilty when it is required. But Mary is not a queen of justice, intent on the punishment of the guilty, but rather a Queen of Mercy, intent only on compassion and pardon for sinners. Accordingly, the Church calls her Queen of Mercy. "These two things which I heard: that power belongs to God, and yours, O Lord, is kindness" (Ps 62:12-13). The Lord has divided the kingdom of God into two parts — justice and mercy. He has reserved the kingdom of justice for himself, and he has granted the kingdom of mercy to Mary. St. Thomas confirms this when he says that the holy Virgin, when she consented to be the Mother of the Redeemer, obtained half of the kingdom of God by becoming queen of mercy, while Jesus remained King of justice.

Albert the Great applies here the history of Queen Esther, who was indeed a type of our Queen Mary. We read in the Book of Esther that in the reign of King Ahasuerus a decree was issued ordering the death of all the Jews. Then Mordecai, who was a Jew, committed their cause to Esther that she might intercede with the king to have the decree revoked. At first Esther refused to do it, fearing that it would make the king more angry. But Mordecai rebuked her and told her that she must not think of saving herself alone, because the Lord had placed her on the throne to obtain salvation for all the Jews. Ahasuerus, when he saw Esther before him, affectionately inquired what she had come to ask him. Then the queen answered, "If I have found favor with you, O king, . . . spare the lives of my people" (Est 7:3). Ahasuerus immediately ordered the sentence to be revoked.

Now if Ahasuerus granted to Esther, because he loved her, the salvation of the Jews, will not God graciously listen to Mary, in his boundless love for her, when she prays to him for those poor sinners who recommend themselves to her, and when she says to him: If I have found favor in your sight, my King and my God, if I have ever found favor with you, give me my people for whom I beg. If you love me, she says to him, give me, my Lord, these sinners for whom I plead. Is it possible that God will refuse her?

Is there anyone who does not know the power of Mary's prayers with God? Every prayer of hers is like a law that mercy shall be given to those for whom she intercedes. St. Bernard asks why the Church names Mary Queen of Mercy. It is because we believe that she obtains the mercy of God for all who seek it, so that not even the greatest sinner is lost if Mary protects him.

But some might think that Mary hesitates in pleading on behalf of some sinners, because she finds them so sinful. Should the majesty and sanctity of this great queen alarm us? No, says St. Gregory, in proportion to her greatness and holiness are her clemency and mercy toward sinners who wish to repent, and have recourse to her. Kings and queens inspire terror by the display of their majesty, and their subjects are afraid to go before them. But what fear, says St. Bernard, can sinners have of going to this Queen of Mercy, since she never shows herself austere to those who seek her, but is always gentle and kind.

Mary Is Our Mother

Not by chance nor in vain do the servants of Mary call her Mother. They cannot invoke her by any other name, and they never weary of calling her Mother; for she is truly the spiritual Mother of our souls and our salvation. Sin, when it deprived our souls of divine grace, also deprived them of life. And when our souls were dead in misery and sin, Jesus came with an excess of mercy and love to restore to us by his death on the Cross that lost life, as he himself declared: "I came that they might have life and have it to the full" (Jn 10:10). "To the full" because, as the theologians teach us, Jesus Christ, by his redemption, brought us blessings greater than the injury Adam inflicted upon us by his sin. He reconciled us to God and thus became the Father of our souls, under the new law of grace, as the prophet Isaiah predicted, "Father-Forever, Prince of Peace" (Is 9:5). But if Jesus is the Father of our souls, Mary is the Mother, for in giving us Jesus, she gave us true life.

At two different times Mary became our spiritual Mother. The first time was when she was found worthy of conceiving in her virginal womb the Son of God. St. Bernardine of Siena teaches us that when the most holy Virgin gave her consent to become Mother of the eternal Word, she, by this very act, demanded of God our salvation. She was so earnestly engaged in obtaining it, that from that time on she carried us, as it were, in her womb like a loving mother. St. Luke says, speaking of the birth of Jesus, that Mary "gave birth to her first-born son" (Lk 2:7). If the evangelist affirms that Mary brought forth her first-born, is it to be supposed that she afterward had other children? But if it is of faith that Mary had no other children according to the flesh except Jesus, then she must have other spiritual children, and these we are. Mary, in bringing forth Jesus who is our Savior and our Life, brought forth all of us to life and salvation.

The second time Mary brought us forth to grace was when, on Calvary, she offered to the Father the life of her Son for our salvation. St. Augustine says that by cooperating with Christ in the birth of the faithful to the life of grace she became the spiritual Mother of all who are members of our Head, Jesus Christ. Mary, to save our souls, was willing to sacrifice the life of her Son. And who was the true soul of Mary but her Jesus, who was her life and all her love? Therefore, Simeon announced to her that her soul would one day be pierced by a sword of sorrows, which was the very spear that pierced the side of Jesus, who was the soul of Mary. And then she in her sorrow brought us forth to eternal life, so that we may all call ourselves children of Mary's sorrows. She, our most loving Mother, was always and entirely united to the divine will. According to St. Bonaventure, when she saw the love of the Father who willed that his Son die for our salvation, and the love of the Son in wishing to die for us, she too, with her whole will, offered her Son and consented that he should die so that we might be saved. Thus she joined herself to that great love of the Father and Son for the human race.

Be joyful, then, all you children of Mary. Remember that she adopts all those who wish her to be their Mother. Joyful: for what fear have you of being lost when this Mother defends and protects you? St. Bonaventure says that everyone who loves this good Mother should take courage. What have we to fear? Our eternal salvation will not be lost, as the final sentence depends upon Jesus our Brother, and upon Mary our Mother. And St. Anselm, full of joy at this thought, exclaims in order to encourage us: "With what certainty may we hope, since our salvation depends upon the sentence of a good brother and a kind mother!"

Hear, then, our mother who calls us and says to us: "Let whoever is simple turn in here" (Prv 9:4). Little children are always saying the word "mother," and in all the dangers which they encounter and in all their fears they cry, "Mother! Mother!" Most sweet Mary, most loving Mother, this is exactly what you wish: that we become little children and always have recourse to you, for you wish to help and save us, as you have saved all your children who have fled to you.

Mary Is Our Life

In order to understand correctly the reason why the Church calls Mary our life, we must consider that as the soul gives life to the body, so divine grace gives life to the soul. For a soul without grace, although nominally alive, in truth is dead. As Mary, by her intercession, obtains for sinners the gift of grace, she restores them to life. The Church applies to her the following words of Proverbs: "Those who seek me find me" (8:17). They find me, or, according to the Septuagint, "They find grace." Thus, to have recourse to Mary is to find the grace of God; for, "He who finds me finds life, and wins favor from the Lord" (Prv 8:35). Listen, as St. Bonaventure comments on these words; listen, all you who desire the kingdom of God. Honor the Virgin Mary, and you shall have life and eternal salvation.

St. Bernard exhorts us, if we have been so unfortunate as to lose divine grace, to strive to recover it, but to strive through Mary; for if we have lost it, she has found it. She is, therefore, called by this saint "the finder of grace." This is what Gabriel meant when he said: "Do not fear, Mary. You have found favor with God." But if Mary had never been without grace, how could the angel say to her that she had found it? A thing is said to be found when it has been lost. The Virgin was always with God and with grace. She was even full of grace, as the archangel himself announced when he greeted her: "Rejoice, O highly favored daughter! The Lord is with you."

If, then, Mary did not find grace for herself, for whom did she find it? She found it for sinners who had lost it. Let sinners, then, who have lost grace flee to Mary. With her they will certainly find it. And let them say: "O Lady, what is lost must be restored to him who has lost it. This grace which you have found is not yours; you have never lost it. It is ours, for we have lost it, and to us you should restore it." If we desire to find the grace of God, let us go to Mary who has found it. She always has been and always will be dear to God; if we have recourse to her, we shall certainly find it. God has placed her in the world to be our defense, and therefore she is ordained to be the mediatrix of peace between the sinner and God.

St. Bernard gives encouragement to the sinner and says: "Go to this Mother of mercy, and show her the wounds which your sins have inflicted on your soul. Then she will surely beg her Son to pardon you, and the Son who loves her so much will certainly hear her." So, too, the Church teaches us to pray to the Lord to grant us Mary's powerful intercession so that we may rise from our sins: "Grant us, merciful God, strength against all our weakness, that we who celebrate the memory of the holy Mother of God may, by the help of her intercession, arise again from our iniquities."

Mary Is Our Sweetness

"He who is a friend is always a friend, and a brother is born for the time of stress" (Prv 17:17). True friends and relatives are not known in times of prosperity but, rather, in times of adversity and misery. Worldly friends do not desert their friend when he is prosperous; but if any misfortune overtakes him, they immediately abandon him. But Mary does not desert her devoted servants.

In our distresses, and especially at the hour of death when our sufferings are the greatest, our good Lady and Mother cannot abandon her faithful servants. As she is our life in the time of our exile, so also she is our sweetness in the hour of death, making sure that it will be sweet and blessed. For since that day on which Mary was present at the death of her Son, Jesus, who was the Head of the elect, she obtained the grace of aiding all the elect at death. Hence, the Church requires that we pray to the Blessed Virgin to aid us, especially in the hour of our death: "Pray for us sinners, now and at the hour of our death."

Mary Is Our Hope

Modern heretics cannot stand the fact that we call Mary our hope: Hail, our hope. They say that God alone is our hope, and that he who places hope in human beings is cursed (Jer 17:5). Mary, they exclaim, is a human being, and, as such, how can she be our hope? Thus say the heretics, but, notwithstanding this, the Church has us invoke Mary by the sweet name of our hope, the hope of all: "Hail, our hope!"

In two ways, says St. Thomas, we can place our hope in a person: as the principal cause, and as the intermediate cause. Those who hope for some favor from a king hope for it from the king as sovereign, or hope for it from one of his ministers as intercessor. If the favor is granted, it comes in the first place from the king; but if it comes through the minister's request, he who has asked the favor justly calls the intercessor his hope. The King of heaven, because he is infinite goodness, desires to enrich us with his graces. But in order to increase our confidence, he has given us his own Mother for our Mother and advocate, and has given her all power to aid us. He, therefore, wishes us to place in her all our hopes of salvation and blessing. Those who place all their hope in creatures without dependence upon God, as sinners do, are certainly cursed by God as Jeremiah says. But those who hope in Mary as Mother of God, powerful to obtain for them graces and life eternal, are blessed and pleasing to God.

Hence, we rightly call Mary our hope, hoping to obtain by her intercession what we could not obtain by our prayers alone. We pray to her, says St. Anselm, so that the dignity of the intercessor will make up for our own deficiencies. Therefore, he adds, to seek Mary's help with such hope is not to distrust the mercy of God, but only to fear our own unworthiness.

Mary Is Our Advocate

There is no doubt, says St. Bernard, that Jesus is the only Mediator between God and man; the God-Man, on account of his merits, can, and according to his promises will, obtain for us pardon and divine grace. But because men recognize and fear the divine Majesty which dwells in him as God, it was necessary that there be another advocate to whom we could have recourse with less fear and more confidence. This is Mary, and we can find no other advocate so powerful with the divine Majesty and so compassionate toward us. We would greatly wrong the mercy of Mary if we should fear to cast ourselves at the feet of this most sweet advocate, who is in all things kind, lovely, and compassionate. Read as much as you will all the history found in the Gospels, and if you find any act of austerity in Mary, then fear to approach her. But you will never find any. Go, then, joyfully to her, for she will save you by her intercession.

Exceedingly beautiful is the prayer of a sinner who has recourse to Mary: "O Mother of my God, I come to you full of confidence. If you reject me, I will plead with you; for in a certain sense you are bound to help me, since all the Church calls you Mother of Mercy. You are so dear to God that he always listens to you. Your great mercy has never failed. Your sweet condescension has never despised any sinner, however enormous his sins, who has had recourse to you. Could the whole Church falsely call you her advocate and the refuge of sinners? No, never let it be said that my sins prevent you, my Mother, from exercising the great office of mercy which you hold. You are at the same time the advocate and mediator of peace between God and man, and, next to your Son, the only hope and secure refuge of sinners. Whatever of grace and glory is yours, even the dignity of being Mother of God, you owe to sinners, since for their sake the divine Word has made you his Mother. Far from you, O divine Mother, be the thought that you should refuse your compassion to any sinner who calls to you. Since, then, Mary, your office is that of peacemaker between God and man, may your great mercy, which far exceeds all my sins, move you to aid me."

Console yourselves, then, you who are fainthearted. I will say with St. Thomas of Villanova: Take heart, you sinners. This great Virgin, who is the Mother of your Judge and God, is the advocate of the human race; powerful and able to obtain whatever she wishes from God; most wise, for she knows every method of appeasing him; universal, for she welcomes all and refuses none.

Mary Is Mercy Itself

St. Bernard, speaking of the great mercy of Mary for us sinners, says that she is the land promised by God, flowing with milk and honey. St. Leo says that to the Virgin such compassion has been given that she not only deserves to be called merciful, but should be called mercy itself. And St. Bonaventure remarks that when he looked on Mary it seemed to him he no longer beheld divine justice, but only divine mercy, with which Mary is filled.

In a word, Mary's mercy is so great that her love can never cease to bring forth for us the fruits of mercy. And what but mercy, exclaims St. Bernard, can flow from a fountain of mercy? For this reason Mary was called the olive tree, "Like a fair olive tree in the field" (Sir 24:14). For as the olive tree produces nothing but oil, the symbol of mercy, thus from the hands of Mary nothing but graces and mercies proceed. If, then, we have recourse to this Mother and ask for the oil of her mercy, we cannot fear that she will refuse us; for she is rich in that oil of mercy. Mary is so full of grace and mercy that there is enough for all.

But why is it said that this fair olive tree is in the field and not, rather, in a garden surrounded by walls and hedges? In order that all may easily see her and easily have recourse to her to obtain mercy. And what more secure refuge can we find, says Thomas à Kempis, than Mary's compassionate heart? There the poor find shelter; the sick, medicine; the afflicted, consolation; the doubtful, counsel; the abandoned, help. Wretched should we be if we did not have this Mother of Mercy, mindful of us in our miseries.

Mary is like Rebekah who, when Abraham's servant asked her for a little water, answered that she would give him water not only for himself but for his camels also (Gn 24:19). Hence St. Bernard, addressing the Blessed Virgin, says: "O Lady, you are more merciful and liberal than Rebekah; therefore, do not be content with dispensing the favors of your unbounded compassion only to the servants of Abraham, the faithful servants of God, but bestow them also on the camels, who represent sinners." And as Rebekah gave more than she was asked, so Mary gives more than we pray for. The liberality of Mary resembles the liberality of her Son, who always gives more than is asked and is said to be "rich in mercy toward all who call upon him" (Rom 10:12).

When the Samaritans refused to receive Jesus Christ and his doctrine, St. James and St. John said to their Master: "Lord, would you not have us call down fire from heaven to destroy them?" (Lk 9:54) But Jesus "turned toward them only to reprimand them" (Lk 9:55), as if he had said, "I am so mild and merciful that I have come from heaven to save, not to punish, sinners; would you wish to see them lost? What fire? What destruction? Be silent, do not speak to me again of punishment; that is not my spirit." We cannot doubt that Mary, whose spirit is in everything so like that of her Son, is wholly inclined to show mercy. This is why Mary was seen clothed with the sun: "A great sign appeared in the sky, a woman clothed with the sun" (Rv 12:1). On this passage St. Bernard remarks, addressing the Virgin: "You have clothed the sun, and are yourself clothed with it. O Lady, you have clothed the Sun, the divine Word, with human flesh, but he has clothed you with his power and his mercy."

So compassionate and kind is this queen when a sinner recommends himself to her mercy that she does not begin to examine his merits and to judge whether he is worthy of being heard, but she graciously hears all and helps them. Hence, Mary is called "beautiful as the moon" (Song 6:10), because as the moon illuminates the smallest bodies upon the earth, so Mary enlightens and helps the most unworthy sinners.

If because of our sins we fear to draw near to God because he is an infinite Majesty that we have offended, we should not hesitate to have recourse to Mary, because in her we shall find nothing to alarm us. She is indeed holy, immaculate, queen of the world, and Mother of God; but she is of our flesh and a child of Adam, like ourselves.

In a word, says St. Bernard, whatever pertains to Mary is full of grace and mercy. For she, as Mother of Mercy, has become all things to all — just and sinners alike — and opens wide the doors to her compassion that all may share it. As the devil prowls about "like a roaring lion looking for someone to devour" (1 Pt 5:8), so, on the contrary, Mary goes about seeking those to whom she can give life and salvation.

II

HER SPECIAL PRIVILEGES

(St. Alphonsus here treats three of Mary's special privileges. His purpose is to inspire

us to love God and have confidence in prayer to Mary.)

Fitness of Mary's Immaculate Conception

It was fitting, first of all, that the eternal Father should create Mary free from the original sin because she was his daughter and his first-born daughter. She herself attests — "Before all ages, in the beginning, he created me" (Sir 24:9) — in a passage that is applied to Mary by the sacred interpreters, by the holy Fathers, and by the Church herself. Whether she is the first-born on account of her predestination together with her Son in the divine decrees before all creatures, or, as others say, the first-born of grace as predestined to be the Mother of the Redeemer after the provision of sin, all agree in calling her the first-born of God. If this is the case, it was not right that Mary should be the slave of the devil, but rather that she should always be possessed by her Creator. Hence, Mary is rightly called the one and only daughter of life, differing in this from others who, being born in sin, are daughters of death.

Moreover, it was right that the eternal Father should create her in his grace, since he destined her to be the restorer of the lost world and mediatrix of peace between man and God. Now certainly he who mediates peace should not be an enemy of the offended person, still less an accomplice of his crime. St. Gregory says that to appease the judge his enemy certainly must not be chosen as an advocate, for instead of appeasing him he would enrage him more. Therefore, as Mary was to be the mediatrix of peace between God and man, there was every reason why she should not appear as a sinner and enemy of God, but as his friend and preserved from sin.

Besides, it was fitting that God should preserve her from original sin, since she was destined to stand in opposition to the devil: "I will put enmity between you and the woman, and between your offspring and hers" (Gn 3:15). Now if Mary was to oppose the devil, surely it was not fitting that she should first be conquered by him and made his slave, but rather that she should be free from every stain and from all subjection to the enemy. Otherwise, as he had in his pride already corrupted the whole human race, he would also have corrupted the pure soul of this Virgin. May the divine Goodness be ever praised for bestowing on her so much grace that she remained free from every stain of sin and could bear him who would crush the devil.

But it was especially fitting that the eternal Father should preserve his daughter from the sin of Adam, because he destined her to be the Mother of his only begotten Son. She was chosen in the mind of God, before every creature, to bring forth God-made-Man. If for no other reason, then, the Father would create her pure from every stain.

St. Thomas says that all things consecrated by God must be holy and pure from every defilement. If David, when he was planning the temple of Jerusalem with a magnificence worthy of the Lord, said: "This castle is not intended for man, but for the Lord God" (1 Chr 29:1), how much more should we believe that the Creator, having destined Mary to be the Mother of his own Son, would adorn her soul with every grace so that it might be a worthy dwelling for a God. Thus the Father could say to this beloved daughter: "As a lily among thorns, so is my beloved among women" (Song 2:2). Daughter among all my other daughters, you are like a lily among thorns. For they are all stained by sin, but you were always immaculate and always my friend.

In the second place, it was befitting the Son that Mary, as his Mother, should be preserved from sin. Other children do not select their own mothers; but if this were ever granted to anyone, who would choose a slave for his mother when he might have a queen, or an enemy of God when he might have a friend of God? If, then, the Son of God alone could select his mother, it is certain that he would choose one befitting a God. And God created her, by the nobility of her nature as well as by the perfection of grace, as a woman suitable to be his mother.

God who is wisdom itself knew how to prepare a fit dwelling for himself. "Wisdom has built her house" (Prv 9:1). How can we think that the Son of God would have chosen to inhabit the soul and body of Mary without first sanctifying her and preserving her from every sin? For, as St. Thomas says, the eternal Word inhabited not only the soul but the body of Mary. The Church prays: Lord, you did not shrink from the Virgin's womb. Indeed, God would have shrunk from becoming flesh in the womb of any other holy virgin, since they were for a time stained with original sin. But he did not shrink from becoming Man in the womb of Mary, because this chosen Virgin was always pure from every guilt and never possessed by the devil. Thus, St. Augustine wrote, the Son of God has built himself no dwelling more worthy than Mary. And St. Cyril of Alexandria asks the question: Who has ever heard of an architect building a house for his own use and then giving the first possession of it to his greatest enemy?

Certainly our Lord, who gave us the command to honor our parents, would not fail when he became Man to observe it himself by bestowing on his Mother every grace and honor. Hence, St. Augustine says that we must certainly believe that Jesus Christ preserved Mary's body from corruption after death, for if he had not done so he would not have observed the law which, as it commands respect to the mother, also condemns disrespect. Jesus would have shown no respect for his Mother's honor if he had not preserved her from original sin.

The tree is known by its fruit. If the Lamb was always immaculate, the Mother must also have been always immaculate. Thus Mary is called the worthy Mother of a worthy Son. None but Mary was the worthy Mother of such a Son, and none but Jesus was the worthy Son of such a Mother.

If, then, it was fitting for the Father to preserve Mary as his daughter from sin, and for the Son because she was his Mother, it was also fitting for the Holy Spirit to preserve her as his spouse. Mary, says St. Augustine, was the only person who merited to be called the Mother and spouse of God. For the Holy Spirit came upon Mary, enriching her with grace beyond all creatures, and dwelt in her and made his spouse Queen of Heaven and Earth. He was with her since he came to form from her immaculate body the immaculate body of Jesus Christ, as the angel predicted — "The Holy Spirit will come upon you and the power of the Most High will overshadow you" (Lk 1:35). For this reason, Mary is called the temple of the Lord and the sanctuary of the Holy Spirit, because by the operation of the Holy Spirit she was made Mother of the incarnate Word.

Now, if an artist were allowed to choose a bride as beautiful or as deformed as he himself could paint her, how great would be his care to make her as beautiful as possible! Who, then, will say that the Holy Spirit did not deal thus with Mary, and that, having it in his power to make his spouse as beautiful as she could be, he did not do so? Yes, it was fitting he should do so.

The bride in the Song of Songs is called "an enclosed garden, a fountain sealed" (Song 4:12). Mary, says St. Jerome, was properly this enclosed garden and sealed fountain, for enemies never entered to harm her. She was always uninjured, remaining holy in soul and body. And St. Bernard also said, addressing the Blessed Virgin, "You are an enclosed garden, where the sinner's hand never entered to rob it of its flowers."

We know that this divine Spouse loved Mary more than all the other saints and angels together. He loved her from the beginning and exalted her in sanctity above all creatures. "Many are the women of proven worth, but you have excelled them all" (Prv. 31:29). If Mary has surpassed all in the riches of grace, she then must have possessed original justice as Adam and the angels had it. "There are . . . maidens without number — one alone is my dove, my perfect one, her mother's chosen, the dear one of her parent" (Song 6:8-9). All just souls are children of divine grace; but among these Mary was the dove without the bitter gall of sin, the perfect one without the stain of original sin, the one conceived in grace. Therefore the angel, before Mary was Mother of God, already found her full of grace, and thus greeted her:

163

"Rejoice, O highly favored daughter." To the other saints grace is given in part, but to the Virgin it was given in fullness. And so St. Thomas says that grace made holy not only the soul but also the flesh of Mary, that with it the Virgin might clothe the eternal Word.

Mary's Humility at the Annunciation

"Whoever exalts himself shall be humbled, but whoever humbles himself shall be exalted" (Mt 23:12). These are the words of our Lord and cannot fail. Therefore God, having determined to make himself Man and being about to choose his Mother on earth, sought among women the holiest and most humble. Among them all he saw one, the youthful Virgin Mary, who was perfect in all virtues, simple, and humble as a dove in her own esteem. "There are . . . maidens without number — one alone is my dove, my perfect one" (Song 6:8-9). Let this one, said God, be my chosen Mother.

Let us now consider how humble Mary was, and how God exalted her: Mary could not humble herself more than she did in the Incarnation of the Word, and God could not exalt Mary more than he has exalted her. For the greater glory and merit of his Mother, the Word did not make himself her Son without first obtaining her consent. Therefore, when the humble young Virgin was in her poor dwelling, the Angel Gabriel came, bearing the great message. He enters and salutes her, saying:

"Rejoice, O highly favored daughter! The Lord is with you. Blessed are you among women" (Lk 1:28). Rejoice, because you are favored above all the other saints. The Lord is with you because you are so humble. You are blessed among women, for all others have been stained by original sin; but you, because you are to be the Mother of the Lord, have been and will always be blessed, and free from every sin.

And what did the humble Mary answer to this greeting of praises? She answered nothing, but she was disturbed by such a greeting: "She was deeply troubled by his words, and wondered what his greeting meant" (Lk 1:29). And why was she disturbed? Through fear of illusion perhaps? No, the text is plain; she was troubled by his words, not by his appearance. Such a disturbance was due to her humility at hearing those praises so exceeding her humble estimate of herself. Thus, the more she is exalted by the angel, the more she humbles herself and the more she considers her nothingness.

But Mary knew from Scripture that a virgin was to be the Mother of the Messiah, and she heard those praises offered by the angel to herself which seemed to belong only to the Mother of God. Did it then come into her mind that perhaps she herself might be that chosen Mother of God? No, her profound humility did not permit this thought. These praises had no other effect than to cause her great fear. Gabriel, seeing Mary so full of fear at that greeting, encouraged her, saying: "Do not fear, Mary. You have found favor with God" (Lk 1:30). Do not be afraid, Mary, nor be surprised by the great titles by which I have saluted you, for if you are so little and humble in your own eyes, God has made you worthy to find the grace lost by man. Therefore he has preserved you from the common stain of all Adam's children. Even from the moment of your conception he has adorned you with a grace greater than that of all the saints. And he now exalts you to be his Mother: "You shall conceive and bear a son and give him the name Jesus" (Lk 1:31).

Now why this delay? The angel, Lady, awaits your answer; or, rather, as St. Bernard says, we who are condemned to death await it. "Behold, Mother," continues St. Bernard, "to you is now offered the price of our salvation, which will be the divine Word in you made Man. If you will accept him for a Son, we shall immediately be delivered from death. Look, the price of our salvation is offered to you. We are freed immediately if you consent. Your Lord himself desires your consent, on which he has made the world's salvation depend." Answer quickly; delay no longer the salvation of the world which now depends on your consent.

But look, Mary already answers. She says to the angel: "I am the servant of the Lord. Let it be done to me as you say" (Lk

1:38). What more beautiful, more humble, more prudent answer could all the wisdom of men have invented, if they had thought for a million years! The answer had no sooner come forth from the humble heart of Mary than it drew from the bosom of the eternal Father the only begotten Son. For hardly had she uttered those words when immediately the Word was made flesh: the Son of God became also the Son of Mary.

Now let us consider the great humility of the Virgin in this answer. She indeed understood how great was the dignity of the Mother of God. She had already been assured by the angel that she was this happy Mother chosen by the Lord. But despite all this, she is not at all raised in her own esteem, and does not stop to enjoy her exaltation. Rather, she considers her own nothingness and the infinite majesty of her God who has chosen her for his Mother. She knows how unworthy she is of such an honor, but would by no means oppose his will.

When her consent is asked, what does she do, what does she say? Wholly annihilated to self, and all inflamed on the other hand with the desire to unite herself more closely to God by entirely abandoning herself to the divine will, she answers, "I am the servant of the Lord." Behold the slave of the Lord, obliged to do whatever her Lord commands. If the Lord chooses me for his Mother, if everything that I have is his gift, then who could think he is selecting me for any merit of my own? "I am the servant of the Lord." What merit can a slave have to be made the Mother of her Lord? "I am the servant of the Lord." Let God alone be praised and not the slave, since it is God's goodness which has led him to glance on a creature so lowly as I am, and thus to make her so great.

In order to comprehend the greatness to which Mary was elevated, it would be necessary to comprehend the majesty of God. It is sufficient to say that God made this Virgin his Mother to have it understood that he could not exalt her more than he did exalt her. By making himself the Son of the Virgin, God established her in a rank superior to that of all the saints and angels.

This explains why the evangelists, who have so fully recorded the praises of others, have been so brief in their descriptions of the privileges of Mary. For it was enough to say that from her Jesus was born. What more would you wish the evangelists to say about the grandeur of this Virgin? Let it be enough that they say she is the Mother of God. Having recorded in these few words her entire merit, it was not necessary for them to describe the particulars separately. And why not? "Because," as St. Anselm answers, "to say only this, that she was the Mother of God, transcends every other glory that can be attributed to her. Whatever name you may wish to call her, whether Queen of Heaven, Ruler of the Angels, or any other title of honor, you will never succeed in honoring her so much as by calling her the Mother of God." But to become Mother of God, it was necessary that the holy Virgin should be exalted to a certain equality with the divine Persons by an infinity of graces. Therefore, if God dwells in creatures in different ways, he dwelt in Mary in a unique way, making himself one with her.

St. Thomas asserts that Mary, being made Mother of God, by reason of this close union with an infinite Good, received a certain infinite dignity. The dignity of the Mother of God is the highest dignity that could be conferred on a mere creature; in this respect, nothing greater can be created. Therefore, St. Bonaventure wrote that God could make a greater world, a greater heaven, but could not exalt a creature to greater excellence than by making her his Mother. But better than all others, Mary herself described the height to which God had elevated her when she said: "God who is mighty has done great things for me" (Lk 1:49).

To conclude, then, this divine Mother is infinitely inferior to God, but immensely superior to all creatures. If it is impossible to find a son more noble than Jesus, it is also impossible to find a mother more noble than Mary. This should cause the servants of such a queen not only to rejoice in her greatness but also to increase their confidence in her most powerful protection. For as Mother of God she has a certain right to his gifts and a right to obtain them for those for whom she prays. God cannot refuse to hear the prayers of this Mother, for he cannot refuse to recognize her as his true and immaculate Mother. So we may pray to Mary by saying:

You prevail with God by a maternal authority; thus even for those who grievously sin you obtain the great grace of reconciliation. For you are always heard, since God in all things conforms to your wishes as to those of a true and pure mother. Therefore, Mother of God and our Mother, in you the power to help us is not lacking. The will, too, is not lacking. For you know that God has not created you for himself alone, but has given you to men as their deliverer. For through you we recover divine grace, and by you the enemy is conquered and crushed.

The Glory of Mary's Assumption
into Heaven

It would seem just that the Church, on this day of the Assumption of Mary into heaven, should invite us to weep rather than to rejoice, since our Mother has left this earth, and we no longer enjoy her presence. As St. Bernard says, it seems that we should rather weep than exult. But, no, holy Church invites us to rejoice: "Let us all rejoice in the Lord, celebrating a feast in honor of the Blessed Virgin Mary." And if we love this Mother, we ought to think more of her glory than of our own particular consolation. What son does not rejoice, although separated from his mother, if he knows that she is going to take possession of a kingdom? Mary today is to be crowned Queen of Heaven, and shall we not celebrate a joyful feast if we truly love her? So, let us rejoice!

After Jesus Christ our Savior had completed the work of our redemption by his death and Resurrection, he ascended into the presence of his Father. Picture how the Savior came from heaven to meet his Mother, and how he said to her, "Arise, my beloved, my beautiful one, and come! For see, the winter is past" (Song 2:10-11). Come, my dear Mother, my beautiful one, leave that valley of tears where you have suffered so much for my love; "Come from Lebanon, my bride, come from Lebanon, come!" (Song 4:8) Come with soul and body to enjoy the reward for your holy life. If you have suffered greatly on earth, far greater is the glory I have prepared for you in heaven. Come there to sit near me, come to receive the crown I will give you as Queen of the Universe.

Now, behold, Mary leaves the earth, and calling to mind the many graces she had there received from her Lord, she looks on it affectionately. And now Jesus offers her his hand and the Blessed Mother rises in the air, passes beyond the clouds and arrives at the gates of heaven. When monarchs make their entrance to take possession of their kingdom, they do not pass through the gates of the city; for either these are taken off entirely or they pass over them. Hence the angels, when Jesus Christ entered paradise, cried: "Lift up, O gates, your lintels; reach up, you ancient portals, that the king of glory may come in!" (Ps 24:7) And now that Mary is going to take possession of the kingdom of the heavens, the angels who accompany her cry to the others who are within: "Lift up, O gates, your lintels; reach up, you ancient portals, that the queen of glory may come in!"

And now Mary enters into the blessed country. But on her entrance the celestial spirits, seeing her so beautiful and glorious, ask of those who are with her, "Who is this coming up from the desert, leaning upon her lover?" (Song 8:5) Who is this creature, so beautiful, that comes from the desert of the earth, a place full of thorns and tribulations? This one comes so pure and so rich in virtue, supported by her beloved Lord. Who is she? The angels who accompany her answer: This is the Mother of our King. She is our queen, the blessed one among women, full of grace, the saint of saints, the beloved of God, the immaculate one, the dove, the most beautiful of all creatures. And then all those blessed spirits begin to bless and praise her, singing, with more reason than the Hebrews sang to Judith, "You are the glory of Jerusalem, the surpassing joy of Israel; You are the splendid boast of our people" (Jdt 15:9). Our Lady and our Queen, you are the glory of paradise, the joy of our heavenly country, you are the honor of us all. Be ever welcome, be ever blessed. We are all your servants, ready for your commands.

If the human mind, says St. Bernard, cannot comprehend the immense glory which God has prepared in heaven for those who have loved him on earth, then who will ever comprehend what he has prepared for her who bore him? On earth he loved her more than all men; and even from the first moment of her creation he loved her more than all men and angels together. Try to imagine the glory he prepared for her. Justly, then, does holy Church sing that Mary, having loved God more than all the angels, has been exalted above them so that she sees no one above her but her Son, who is the only begotten Son of God.

The glory of Mary, which was full and complete, is different from that which the other saints have in heaven. It is true that in heaven all the blessed enjoy perfect peace and full contentment. Yet it will always be true that none of them enjoys that glory which he could have merited if he had loved and served God with greater fidelity. Therefore, although the saints in heaven desire nothing more than what they possess, yet in fact there is something more they *could* desire. It is also true that the sins which they have committed and the time which they have lost do not bring suffering. But it cannot be denied that the most good done in life gives the greatest contentment.

Mary in heaven desires nothing and has nothing to desire. Which of the saints in paradise, says St. Augustine, if asked whether or not he has committed sins, can answer no, except Mary? It is certain, as the Council of Trent has defined, that Mary never committed any sin, not even the slightest. She never did an action that was not meritorious. She never said a word or had a thought or drew a breath that was not directed to the greatest glory of God. In a word, she never relaxed or stopped one moment in her onward course to God. She never lost anything through negligence, for she always cooperated with grace with all her power and loved God as much as she could love him. O Lord, she now says to him in heaven, if I have not loved you as much as you deserve, at least I have loved you as much as I could.

Let us rejoice, then, with Mary in the exalted throne to which God has elevated her in heaven. And let us rejoice also for her own sake, since if our Mother has ceased to be present with us by rising in glory to heaven, she has not ceased to be present with us in her affection. No, being nearer and more united to God, she knows our miseries better and therefore pities them more and is better able to relieve us. And will you, O Blessed Virgin, because you have been so exalted in heaven, forget us? No, may God preserve us from the thought. A heart so merciful cannot but pity our miseries. If the pity of Mary for us was so great when she lived upon earth, how much greater, says St. Bonaventure, is it in heaven where she now reigns.

And with this love of our Mother Mary, I leave you, my readers, saying to you: Continue joyfully to honor and love this good Lady. Try also to promote the love of her wherever you can; and do not doubt that, if you persevere in true devotion to Mary, even until death, your salvation is assured. I finish, not because I have nothing more to say about the glories of this great queen, but so that I may not tire you. The little I have written may indeed be enough to show you the great value of devotion to the Mother of God. I wish to see you safe and holy, to see you become a loving and devoted child of this most lovable queen. And if you know that this book has helped you somewhat, I ask you, in your charity, recommend me to Mary, and ask of her the grace which I ask for you — that we may both meet in paradise at her feet, together with all her other dear children.

prayers

of

st alphonsus

INTRODUCTION

God has set his heart on saving us. "He wants all men to be saved" (1 Tm 2:4). And he is ready to give all the help necessary for salvation, but as St. Augustine says, "He gives only to those who ask." Thus it is a common opinion of theologians that prayer is necessary for adults as a means of salvation. A person who does not pray, and who neglects to ask for the help required to overcome temptations and to preserve graces already received, cannot be saved.

On the other hand, our Lord cannot refuse to give graces to those who ask for them, because he has promised to do so: "Call to me, and I will answer you" (Jer 33:3). Ask me, and I will not fail to hear you. This promise is not to be understood with reference to temporal goods, because God only gives these when they are for the good of the soul. But he has promised absolutely to give spiritual graces to anyone who asks him, and having promised it, he is obliged to give them to us.

Notice that, while on God's part prayer is a promise, on our part it is a binding precept: "Ask, and you will receive" (Mt 7:7). "He told them a parable on the necessity of praying always" (Lk 18:1). These words convey a command which is binding for our whole life, but especially when a man is in danger of death or of falling into sin; for if he does not then have recourse to God, he will certainly be lost. And he who has already fallen commits another sin when he does not turn to God for help.

But will God hear him while he is still in sin? Yes, he does hear, if the sinner humbles himself and prays for pardon; for it is written in the Gospel, "Whoever asks, receives" (Lk 11:10). God, then, has promised to hear all who pray to him, whether they are just or sinners. In another place, God says, "Call upon me in time of distress; I will rescue you" (Ps 50:15).

No, there will be no excuse on the day of judgment for anyone who dies in mortal sin. It will be of no use for him to say that he did not have the strength to resist the temptation which troubled him, because Jesus Christ will answer: If you did not have the strength, why did you not ask for it? I should certainly have given it to you.

You see, then, that if you want to be saved and keep yourself in the grace of God, you must often pray to him. The Council of Trent declares that for a man to persevere in God's grace, it is not enough that he should have only that general aid which God gives to all men; he must also have that special assistance which can only be obtained by prayer. For this reason all the Doctors of the Church say that everyone is bound, under serious sin, to pray often to God.

It is also most useful to practice some particular devotion to the Mother of God, who is called the Mother of perseverance. A person who does not have this special devotion to the Blessed Virgin will find it very difficult to persevere; for St. Bernard says that all divine graces, and especially this one of perseverance, come to us through Mary.

Therefore, I repeat: If you wish to be saved, pray continually to the Lord to give you light and strength not to fall into sin. Every morning ask him to keep you from sin during that day. And when any bad thought or occasion of sin presents itself to your mind, immediately have recourse to Jesus Christ and the Blessed Virgin, and say, "Jesus, help me! Most Blessed Virgin, come to my aid!" It is enough at such a time to utter the names of Jesus and Mary, and the temptation may vanish; but should the temptation continue, persevere in seeking the assistance of Jesus and Mary, and you will be victorious.

Act of Faith

O God, I believe that you are my God, the Creator of all things; that you reward the just with an eternal paradise and punish the wicked in hell for all eternity. I believe that you are one in being and three in persons, Father, Son, and Holy Spirit. I believe in the Incarnation and death of Jesus Christ. I believe, in short, all that the Church believes. I thank you for having made me a Christian, and I will live and die in this holy faith.

Act of Hope

O God, trusting in your promises because you are powerful, faithful, and merciful, I hope through the merits of Jesus Christ to obtain pardon for my sins, final perseverance, and the glory of heaven.

Act of Love and Contrition

O God, because you are infinite goodness, worthy of infinite love, I love you with all my heart above all things; and for love of you, I love my neighbor also. I repent with all my heart, and am sorry for all my sins, because by them I have offended your infinite goodness. I resolve, by the help of your grace, rather to die than ever to offend you again.

Prayer to Obtain Final Perseverance

Eternal Father, I humbly adore and thank you for having created me and for having redeemed me. I thank you for having made me a Christian by giving me the true faith and for adopting me as your child in Baptism. I thank you for having given me time to repent after my many sins, and for having pardoned all my offenses. I renew my sorrow for them, because I have displeased you. I thank you also for having preserved me from falling again, as I would have done if you had not held me up and saved me. But my enemies do not cease fighting against me, nor will they until I die. If you do not help me continually, I will lose your grace again. I, therefore, pray for perseverance till death. Your Son Jesus has promised that you will give us whatever we ask for in his name. By the merits of Jesus Christ, I beg you, for myself and for all those who are in your grace, the grace of never more being separated from your love. May we always love you in this life and in the next. Mary, Mother of God, pray to Jesus for me.

Prayer to Obtain Constancy in Prayer

Eternal Father, for the love of Jesus Christ, let me never fail to recommend myself to you whenever I am tempted. I know you always help me when I have recourse to you; but my fear is that I may forget to recommend myself to you, and so my negligence will be the cause of my ruin. By the merits of Jesus Christ, give me grace to pray to you. But grant me such an abundant grace that I may always pray, and pray as I ought! My Mother Mary, whenever I have had recourse to you, you have obtained for me the help which has kept me from falling! Now I come to beg you to obtain a still greater grace, that of recommending myself always to your Son and to you in all my times of need. My queen, you obtain all you desire from God by the love you bear for Jesus Christ. Obtain for me now this grace which I beg of you: to pray always and never to cease praying until I die. Amen.

Prayer for the Graces
Necessary for Salvation

Eternal Father, your Son has promised that you will grant us all the graces which we ask for in his name. In the name and merits of Jesus Christ, I ask the following graces for myself and for all mankind.

Please give me a lively faith in all that the Church teaches. Enlighten me that I may know the vanity of the goods of this world and the immensity of the infinite good that you are. Make me also see the deformity of the sins I have committed, that I may humble myself and detest them as I should.

Give me a firm confidence of receiving pardon for my sins, holy perseverance, and the glory of heaven, through the merits of

Jesus Christ and the intercession of Mary.

Give me a great love for you that will detach me from the love of this world and of myself, so that I may love none other but you.

I beg of you a perfect resignation to your will. I offer myself entirely to you, that you might do with me and all that belongs to me as you please.

I beg of you a great sorrow for my sins.

I ask you to give me the spirit of true humility and meekness, that I may accept with peace and even with joy all the contempt, ingratitude and ill-treatment I may receive. At the same time, I also ask you to give me perfect charity, which shall make me wish well to those who have done evil to me.

Give me love for the virtue of mortification, by which I may chastise my rebellious senses and oppose my self-love. Give me a great confidence in the Passion of Jesus Christ and in the intercession of Mary immaculate. Give me a great love for the Blessed Sacrament, and a tender devotion and love to your holy Mother. Give me, above all, holy perseverance and the grace always to pray for it, especially in time of temptation and at the hour of death.

Finally, I recommend to you the holy souls of purgatory, my relatives and benefactors, and in a special manner I recommend to you all those who hate me or who have in any way offended me; I beg you to render them good for the evil they have done or may wish to do me. Grant that, by your goodness, I may come one day to sing your mercies in heaven; for my hope is in the merits of your blood and in the patronage of Mary. Mary, Mother of God, pray to Jesus for me.

Prayer before Confession

God of infinite majesty, behold at your feet a traitor who has offended you over and over again, but who now humbly seeks forgiveness. Lord, do not reject me; "A heart contrite and humbled, O God, you will not spurn" (Ps 51:19). I thank you for having waited for me until now and for not letting me die in sin. Since you have waited for me, my God, I hope that by the merits of Jesus Christ you will pardon me in this confession for all the offenses I have committed against you. I repent and am sorry for them, because by them I have merited hell and lost heaven. But it is not so much on account of hell, but because I have offended you, that I am sorry from the bottom of my heart. I love you, my supreme Good, and because I love you, I repent of all the insults I have offered you. I have turned my back on you; I have despised your grace and your friendship. Lord, I have lost you by my own free will. Forgive me all my sins for the love of Jesus Christ, now that I repent with all my heart. I resolve for the future, by your grace, never more willingly to offend you. Yes, my God, I would rather die than ever sin again.

Prayer after Confession

My dear Jesus, how much I owe you! By the merits of your blood I have this day been pardoned. I thank you. You deserve all my love. I will give it all to you. I will no longer separate myself from you. I have promised you this already; now I repeat my promise of being ready to die rather than offend you again. I promise also to avoid all occasions of sin. My Jesus, you know my weakness; give me grace to be faithful to you until death and to have recourse to you when I am tempted. Most holy Mary, help me. You are the Mother of perseverance; I place my hope in you.

Prayer to Our Lord
in the Blessed Sacrament

My Lord Jesus Christ, because you love us so much, you remain night and day in this sacrament, full of pity and love, awaiting, calling, and welcoming all who come to visit you. I believe that you are present in the sacrament of the altar. I adore you from the depths of my heart. I thank you for the many graces you have given me, and especially for having given me yourself in this sacrament, for having given me Mary your Mother as my advocate, and for having called me to visit you here. I speak to your most amiable and loving heart for three reasons: to thank you for this great gift; to atone for all the insults which you have received; and to compensate by my adoration the lack of it in all those places where the Blessed Sacrament is the least reverenced and most abandoned. My Jesus, I love you with my whole heart. I am sorry that I have so often offended your infinite goodness. With the help of your grace, I resolve to offend you no more. I now consecrate myself entirely to you. I give you my will, my affections, my desires, and all that is mine; do with me and with all that belongs to me whatever you wish. I ask for nothing but your holy love, final perseverance, and the perfect fulfillment of your will. I recommend to you the souls in purgatory, especially those who were most devoted to this sacrament and to Mary. I also recommend to you all poor sinners. And lastly, my beloved Savior, I unite all my affections with those of your most loving heart, and thus united, I offer them to your eternal Father, and in your name I beg him to accept and grant them.

Prayer to the Blessed Virgin

Most holy immaculate Virgin Mary, my Mother, I, the most miserable of sinners, kneel before you, the advocate, the hope, and the refuge of sinners. I venerate you, great queen, and I thank you for the many favors you have already obtained for me, especially for having saved me from hell which I have so often deserved. I love you, most amiable Lady, worthy of all love. And because I love you, I promise to serve you always, and to do everything in my power to make others serve you also. In you I hope; I place my salvation in your hands. Accept me for your servant; receive me under your mantle, Mother of Mercy. You are all-powerful with God. Free me, then, from all temptations, or at least obtain for me the strength to conquer them as long as I live. From you I seek a genuine love of Jesus Christ. With your help I hope to die a good death. I beseech you, Mother, to help me always, but especially at the last moment of my life. Do not leave me until you see me safe in heaven, blessing you and singing your mercies for all eternity.

Prayer to Jesus and Mary for the Grace of a Good Death

My Lord Jesus Christ, by that bitterness which you endured on the Cross when your soul was separated from your sacred body, have pity on my sinful soul when it leaves my body to enter into eternity.

Mary, by that sorrow which you experienced on Calvary, obtain for me a good death, that loving Jesus and you in this life, I may reach heaven where I shall love you both for all eternity.

Prayerful Reflections to Stimulate God's Love in Our Hearts

God is a treasury of all grace, of all good, of all perfection.

God is infinite, God is eternal, God is immense, God is unchangeable.

God is powerful, God is wise, God is provident, God is just.

God is merciful, God is holy, God is beautiful, God is brightness itself, God is rich, God is all things. He is, therefore, worthy of all our love.

God is infinite; he gives to all and needs nothing from anyone. All that we have comes to us from God, but God is sufficient in himself.

God is eternal; he has always been eternal and always will be. We can count the years and the days of our existence, but God knows no beginning and will never have an end.

God is immense, and is essentially present in every place. We, when we are in one place, cannot be in another. But God is in all places, in heaven, on earth, in the sea, outside us, and within us. "Where can I go from your spirit? from your presence where can I flee? If I go up to the heavens, you are there; if I sink to the nether world, you are present there" (Ps 139:7-8).

God is unchangeable, and all that he has ordained by his holy will from eternity, he wills now and will do so forever. "Surely I, the Lord, do not change" (Mal 3:6).

God is powerful; and in comparison with God, all the power of creatures is but weakness.

God is wise; and in comparison with God, all human wisdom is ignorance.

God is provident; and in comparison with God, all human foresight is ridiculous.

God is just; and in comparison with God, all human justice is defective.

God is merciful; and in comparison with God, all human clemency is imperfect.

God is holy; in comparison with God, all human sanctity, though it be heroic, falls short in an infinite degree: "None is good but God alone" (Lk 18:19).

God is beauty itself; and in comparison with God, all human beauty is deformity.

God is brightness itself; and in comparison with God, all other brightness, even that of the sun, is darkness.

God is rich; and in comparison with God, all human wealth is poverty.

God is all things; and in comparison with God, the highest, most sublime, most admirable of created things are nothing. He is, therefore, worthy of so much love that all the angels and all the saints of heaven do nothing but love God, and will throughout all eternity be occupied only in loving him. And in this love of God, they are and will be always happy.